100 Literacy Hours

YEAR 3

Published by Scholastic Ltd,
Villiers House,
Clarendon Avenue,
Leamington Spa,
Warwickshire CV32 5PR

© 1998 Scholastic Ltd

AUTHOR
Chris Webster

EDITORS
Lorna Gilbert
Irene Goodacre

ASSISTANT EDITOR
Lesley Sudlow

SERIES DESIGNER
Joy White

COVER ARTWORK
Val Biro

ILLUSTRATIONS
Robin Lawrie

© 1998 Scholastic Ltd Text © 1998
2 3 4 5 6 7 8 9 8 9 0 1 2 3 4 5 6 7

British Library Cataloguing-in-Publication Data
A catalogue record for this book is available from the British Library.

ISBN 0-590-53877-2

Contents

ACKNOWLEDGEMENTS

The publishers gratefully acknowledge permission to reproduce the following copyright material:

Aladdin Books for the use of text and illustrations from *All Ways of Looking At: The Seashore* by Jane Walker Illustrations © 1993, Justine Peek and David Marshall Text © 1993, Jane Walker, (1993, Aladdin Books).

Book Tokens Ltd for the adaptation of a Book Tokens Ltd advertisement and the use of the Book Tokens Ltd logo © Book Tokens Ltd.

Controller of HMSO for the use of the MetFAX map, table and symbols issued on 27 February 1998 reproduced from information supplied by The Met Office © Crown copyright, by permission of the Controller of HMSO.

Wes Magee for 'School Daze' by Wes Magee from *Scholastic Collections: Poetry* compiled by Wes Magee © 1992, Wes Magee (1992, Scholastic Ltd).

Penguin Ltd for the use of illustrations from *Dustbin Charlie* by Ann Pilling Illustration © 1988, Jean Baylis (1988, Viking Kestrel).

Random House UK Ltd for the use of extracts from *A Necklace of Raindrops* by Joan Aiken © 1968, Joan Aiken (1968, Jonathan Cape).

John Rice for the use of 'Conversation at the school dinner table' from *Zoomballoonistic* by John Rice © 1982, John Rice (1982, Aten Press).

Scholastic Inc, New York for the use of 'Pizza Pizzazz' by Liza Charlesworth from *Instant Activities For Poetry that Kids Really Love!* edited by Linda Beech © 1997, Liza Charlesworth (1997, Scholastic Inc) and extract from *Swimming with Sea Lions* by Ann McGovern © 1992, Ann McGovern (1992, Scholastic Inc).

Scholastic Ltd for the use of 'Rocket Poem' by Michael Rosen from *Mind Your Own Business* by Roger McGough © 1974, Michael Rosen (1974, André Deutsch).

Sony Music Publishing for the use of lyrics to *I'm Only Sleeping* by John Lennon and Paul McCartney © Lennon and McCartney.

Walker Books Ltd for the use of an extract from *Robin Hood and the Sherriff* by Julian Atterton © 1995, Julian Atterton (1995, Walker Books).

David Whitehead for the use of his poem 'Rainbow' from *Scholastic Collections: Poetry* compiled by Wes Magee © 1992, David Whitehead (1992, Scholastic Ltd).

Every effort has been made to trace copyright holders and the publishers apologize for any inadvertent omissions.

Introduction

INTRODUCTION

ABOUT THE SERIES

100 Literacy Hours is a series of year-specific teachers' resource books that provide a core of material for the teaching of the English curriculum within the context of the National Literacy Strategy *Framework for Teaching* and within the structure of the Literacy Hour. Each book offers term-by-term lesson plans, complete with objectives and organization grids and accompanied, where relevant, with photocopiable texts and activity sheets. The materials are ready-to-use, and their adaptable format enables them to be used as flexibly as possible. The 100 hours provided offer a balance of both reading and writing, and of range: fiction and poetry and non-fiction. However, it is expected that you will wish to personalize the material – altering the order, interleaving lessons plans with complementary materials from your school's existing schemes, consolidating work by using the structure of a lesson plan as a model for a lesson with different content, and so on. The loose-leaf format of each book, with hole-punched, perforated, tear-out pages, makes the integration of other tried-and-tested and favourite material into the core very easy.

USING THIS BOOK

The materials

This book provides 100 literacy hours for Year 3, presented as 'units' of between 1 and 5 hours. There is a balance of reading and writing units, most of which are linked in order to demonstrate and reinforce the close relationship. The bulk of the 100 hours is fully supported with detailed lesson plans and integrated photocopiable resources. The remainder of the hours are plans for suitable follow-on or follow-up hours linked to some of the units. These can be found at the back of the book in the section called 'Follow-up' (see page 202) and are presented as grids outlining objectives and organization. Together, these materials should be regarded as a core, as a starting point for developing your own personalized folder for the year.

Adapting and personalizing the materials

During the trialling of these resources, wide differences in ability were found in classes of the same year group in different schools. This means that the *precise* content of the plans and resources will almost certainly need modification to suit the children in a particular school. One way to do this is as follows:
■ Separate the pages of the book and place them in an A4 ring-binder.
■ Adjust the level of the photocopiable resource sheets to match the needs of the children in your year group.
■ 'Trade' materials with higher or lower year groups so that the average level matches that of the target year group.
■ Add your own favourite teaching materials in the appropriate places.
■ Substitute materials for others if necessary (for example, if you have a set of books which you wish to use instead of one of the ones recommended).
   You have now created a tailor-made folder of plans and resources for your year group!

Preparing a scheme of work

All schools are required to write detailed schemes of work, and these materials have been designed to facilitate this process.
   The termly Overview grids provided on pages 16–21 have been compiled by extracting the 'Objectives' grids from each teaching unit and putting them together to provide you with what are, essentially, medium-term plans. These grids are photocopiable so, should you wish to alter the order of units and/or add your own, they can be copied, cut and pasted to make your own plans. On page 22 there are also photocopiable blank objectives grids for you to use when inserting your own material.

ORGANIZATION OF TEACHING UNITS

Each term is divided into teaching units comprising between 1–5 hours. Each of the main units has either a reading or a writing focus (although there is, of course, overlap) and a fiction, poetry or non-fiction content.

The units are organized as follows:

OBJECTIVES GRID

Outlines the word-, sentence- and text-level objectives of the unit.

UNIT	SPELLING/VOCABULARY	GRAMMAR/PUNCTUATION	COMPREHENSION/ COMPOSITION
READING POETRY Classic poem: 'The Months of the Year' by Sara Coleridge.	Recognize one- and two-syllable rhymes. Spell the months of the year.	Use grammatical knowledge to reassemble text. Revise adjectives.	Identify couplets. Demonstrate comprehension by resequencing.

ORGANIZATION GRID

Outlines the key activities for each part of each hour.

	INTRODUCTION	WHOLE-CLASS SKILLS WORK	DIFFERENTIATED GROUP ACTIVITIES	CONCLUSION
HOUR 1	Read 'The Months of the Year' on photocopiable page 58.	Investigate rhyme. Introduce the term 'couplet'. Identify couplets in the poem.	1–3: Resequence a cut-up version of the poem. 4*: Resequence a simpler cut-up version of the poem.	Re-read the poem. Selected pupils recite part of the poem from memory.
HOUR 2	Re-read 'The Months of the Year'.	Spell the months of the year. Revise adjectives. Find adjectives in the poem.	1*: Write own second line to each verse. 2 & 3: Add adjectives in blank spaces. 4*: As above, but with teacher support.	Selected pupils read out their own version of the poem.

UNIT LESSON PLANS

Each unit of lesson plans is written to the following headings:

Resources

Provides a list of what you need for teaching the whole unit.

Preparation

Outlines any advance preparation needed before the hour(s) begins.

Synopsis

Gives a synopsis of the story, where whole published fiction texts are used as the basis of units.

Each hour is then set out as follows:

Introduction

Sets out what to do in the whole-class shared reading/writing session.

Whole-class skills work

Sets out what to do in the whole-class word- and sentence-level skills sessions. (See page 11 for further information about whole-class skills work.)

Differentiated group activities

Sets out what each group does in the guided group and independent work session. (See page 12 for further information about differentiated group work.)

Conclusion

Sets out what to do in the whole-class plenary session.

Follow-up

Some units lend themselves particularly to follow-up hours and these are indicated in the lesson plans and cross-referenced to the section at the back of the book.

Further ideas

Provides ideas for extending what is done within the hours of the unit.

Photocopiable sheets

Photocopiable resource and activity sheets that support each unit. These can be found at the end of each relevant unit and are marked with the photocopiable symbol

Many of the sheets have more than one application and are therefore used in several units.

READING UNITS

These teaching units have three aims:
■ to develop basic reading skills across a wide range of texts – fiction, poetry and non-fiction
■ to develop skills of comprehension, inference, deduction and literary appreciation
■ to encourage enjoyment of reading.

Using the texts

All shorter texts are provided on the photocopiable resource sheets. The following longer texts will be needed (half-class sets are recommended for fiction and group sets for non-fiction):
■ *Dustbin Charlie* by Ann Pilling, Young Puffin, ISBN 0-14-032391-0
■ *Dustbin Charlie Cleans Up* by Ann Pilling, Young Puffin, ISBN 0-14-036406-4 (optional, for Follow-up)
■ *A Necklace of Raindrops* by Joan Aiken & Jan Pienkowski, Puffin, ISBN 0-14-030754-0
■ *The Seashore* by Jane Walker, Aladdin Books/ Watts Books, ISBN 0-7496-1450-1
■ *Robin Hood and the Sheriff* by Julian Atterton, Walker Books, ISBN 0-7445-2490-3.

All the texts are intended for use as *shared texts*; that is to say, texts for whole-class and/or guided group reading. Use of appropriate teaching methods enables children to read and understand texts beyond their *independent* reading level. These methods include:
■ preparation, for example giving the background to a story, prior study of difficult words
■ an initial reading to the whole class with children following the text
■ re-reading in groups with less able groups supported by the teacher
■ differentiated follow-up activities which allow more able children to respond independently to the text while further support is given to less able readers
■ guided reading, in which the teacher takes children through the text helping them with phonic or contextual clues (less able readers), or higher-level reading skills (more able readers).

Additional suggestions are given, where relevant, in the detailed lesson plans, for example use of different versions of the same story.

It is assumed that children will be following a programme of guided reading alongside their reading of these shared texts.

Managing the reading of longer texts

In those units where the whole of longer texts is read, it is assumed that sometimes the chunks of reading allocated to the Introduction session (whole-class shared reading) may need to be undertaken outside of the session or lesson time. It could be included in guided group reading, or in other shared reading time or as homework. Recording and making copies of an audio tape of the text will enable those children who cannot read the text independently to have access to the story.

Responding to texts

Since the mid-1980s, a complete methodology for teaching children how to respond to texts has developed, and is becoming well established from KS1 to KS4. The materials in this book try to exemplify as many types of responses as possible, so that, as well as providing specific lessons, they also offer models which can be adapted for use with other texts. Some examples of responses to texts are:

- cloze – fill in gaps in a text
- sequencing – place a cut-up text in order
- design a storyboard – such as plan a film version of the text
- use drama techniques to explore a text – for example role-play, hot-seating
- design a newspaper front page about an aspect of the text
- comprehension questions answered orally or in writing.

Written comprehension

The majority of written tasks set in these materials encourage a creative response to reading. These often reveal children's comprehension of the text as clearly as any formal comprehension, and, like the oral and dramatic activities, they are just as effective in developing comprehension skills. However, children do need to practise formal written comprehension of different kinds, and activities for this have been provided in many of the units. Note that the main purpose of the comprehension material is to develop understanding of the texts, not to provide detailed numerical assessments. Marking should therefore be kept simple. On most occasions, the marking can be done orally in a concluding session. You might take each question in turn, asking for responses from the children and discussing them. The correct answer (or answers) can then be identified and the children can mark their own answers, simply placing a tick if they have got it right. Queries can be dealt with immediately. You can look at the comprehensions later to see at a glance which children are doing well at basic recall, which are doing well at inference and deduction, and most important of all, which children are struggling with basic understanding. These children should then be given further support during the next guided reading session.

WRITING UNITS

These units provide a series of structured writing experiences throughout the year leading to a more integrated, creative and open-ended approach in Term 3 which draws together and puts into practice previous skills taught and developed. The idea is to provide 'props' for learning and then to remove them gradually in the hope that children will be able to write with increasing independence and creativity. Examples of

props are the many 'templates' to support writing. These include sentence and paragraph prompts for fiction, and page-layout templates for certain types of non-fiction (see 'Words in Windows' unit, Term 3). Other kinds of props are the Story Planner (see 'Myth-maker' unit, Term 2) and the Redrafting Checklist (see 'Proverbs' unit, Term 3). Regular use of these will help children to internalize the prompts they contain, and so help them build independence as writers. Towards the end of Term 3, the 'Writing Simulation' unit provides a context for children to write in a range of forms for a range of purposes and audiences, so bringing together in a creative way, the wide range of skills covered throughout the year.

Cross-curricular writing

The best opportunities for most non-narrative writing occur in other curriculum areas. Therefore, when the necessary skills have been introduced through one of the non-fiction units, they should be applied to another curriculum area soon afterwards. It would be well worth holding year-group meetings specifically to 'map' opportunities for non-narrative writing across the curriculum.

REFERENCE AND RESEARCH SKILLS UNITS

Within each term there are two 1-hour Reference and Research Skills units. The purpose of these units is to focus attention on important skills that may otherwise not get appropriate time within the context of other lesson plans. In this book for Year 3, the Reference and Research Skills units deal with the following skills:
Term 1:
Using a thesaurus.
Understanding the distinction between fact and fiction.
Term 2:
Dictionary work (alphabetical order; front, middle, back of dictionary work).
Making notes.
Term 3:
Further dictionary work (features of an entry).
Library classification systems.

WORD PLAY UNITS

At the end of each term there is a Word Play unit. The purpose of these units is to demonstrate that playing with words is not only 'OK' and fun, but also a powerful learning tool. The Word Play units for Year 3 deal with the following:
Term 1:
Reading and writing shape poems.
Term 2:
Re-writing well-known nursery rhymes.
Term 3:
Using poetry to investigate humorous ways of depicting speech and to explore the reading of nonsense words by breaking them down into syllables.

10

SPEAKING AND LISTENING

Speaking and listening is also an essential part of literacy, and development of skills in this important area has been integrated into the units for both reading and writing. Speaking and listening is *the* most important way of developing higher-order reading skills. Children must be able to explore texts through discussion, role-play and other forms of oral 'comprehension' before they can do justice to more formal written comprehension. 'Brainstorming' sharing ideas, helping each other to check work and so on, will all help children to write more effectively. The challenge for the teacher is to ensure that this discussion is clearly focussed on the task and not merely idle chatter.

TIMING OF THE LITERACY HOUR

A brisk pace is an important feature of an effective Literacy Hour. The following suggestions, based on experience in trialling these materials, will help to keep things moving:

■ Train pupils in efficient classroom routines (see below under 'Differentiated group activities').

■ Don't talk too much! Keep explanations brief. Get children on task as soon as possible, and give further clarification and help in the context of the activity.

■ Don't let skills sessions overrun, unless there is a good reason which has been previously planned for. Skills will be revised and practised several times throughout the year within the context of other slots in the Literacy Hour and outside of it.

■ When starting group activities sessions, give a clear message about what you want children to have achieved in the time allocated, and encourage them to work efficiently such as not wasting time decorating a border before starting writing and so on.

Introductory session

Most often, these sessions involve the reading aloud of a shared text. Where possible, children should follow the reading in their own copy of the text. Using an overhead projector is the best way of doing this (see below). It allows a shared text to be used as a focal point for the whole class in the same way as a Big Book. Find ways to make them interactive by involving children in reading, asking questions and so on. Give appropriate background information and briefly discuss vocabulary and ideas. However, in all this, do not lose sight of the need to keep the pace of the lesson moving!

Whole-class skills work

It is during these sessions that the majority of grammar, punctuation, spelling and phonic skills are taught. The main principle is that the skills arise from the shared text and will also be used in the related writing unit. Over the year, key skills should be revisited many times so that children's mastery of them will grow incrementally. A word of warning: many grammatical concepts are difficult and abstract, so do not expect children to grasp them all at once. Expect it to be a slow process in which their understanding develops over several years. For example, many children may not achieve mastery of writing in paragraphs until they reach their teens – but they will not achieve it at all if a start is not made when they are much younger.

Although the materials in this book include spelling activities based on spelling rules and patterns arising from the texts, they cannot take the place of a programme of individualized spelling for children. Children could collect a list of words they need to learn in a spelling book. This could be supplemented at least once a week with

words from a standard list to make a list of, say, ten (or more for more able/older children). Children then learn their lists using the LOOK/SAY/COVER/WRITE/CHECK method. Pairs of children can test each other on their own lists. Any words not learned can be carried over into the next list.

The same book can be used backwards to collect new items of vocabulary. Again, these should be a mixture of words which children have come across themselves, and words introduced during teaching (for example, character adjectives, synonyms of 'said').

Differentiated group activities

For most group activities, three levels of differentiation are suggested, usually shown as four groups to reflect a normal distribution of ability:

Group 1:	above average pupils.
Groups 2 & 3:	average pupils.
Group 4:	below average pupils.

In the average KS2 class, group sizes would be between 7–8 (with some trade-off between groups according to the spread of ability in the class). This is fine for organizational purposes, and working with the teacher, but too large for most collaborative activities. These groups will therefore need to be subdivided into smaller groups of fours or pairs for many activities. There will also be occasions when mixed-ability groups are most appropriate for the activities (for example, the drama units).

Children need to know which main group they are in and be able to subdivide into fours or pairs quickly and efficiently. To help this process, teachers could name the groups, for example 'Home Group', 'Small Groups', 'Pairs', and train children to get into the appropriate group immediately the group is named.

When this routine is firmly established, children should then be given the experience of working with children from other groups, for example opposite sex pairs, fours made up of pairs from different 'Home Groups' and so on. It is also important to give them the experience of working in mixed-ability groups for appropriate activities.

The teacher should try to divide teaching time equally between all groups over the course of the week – the more able need help just as much as the less able if they are given suitably demanding tasks.

[NB: An asterisk (*) after the group number is used on the grids and in the lesson plans to show which groups the teacher should be working with during the group activities session.]

Finally, it is important to stress that even when a teacher is working intensively with one group, the first priority is always the overall work rate of the whole class. The following tips will help:

■ Train children to work independently. Tell them that you cannot help them while you are working with a group – their turn will come. In the meantime, they must find out for themselves, or ask a friend or a classroom assistant.

■ When working with a group, sit in a position so that the rest of the class can be seen.

■ Break off group work immediately to deal with lazy or disruptive children. They will soon learn that they are under supervision even when you are working with a group.

Concluding sessions

The key objective in most of these sessions is to review the teaching points of the lesson and ensure that the work of *selected* children, pairs or groups is shared with the class for discussion and evaluation. Enough should be heard to exemplify the variety of work produced, but not so much that it becomes boring, or takes too much time. Keep a record of who has presented what to ensure that all children have the opportunity to present their work in due course.

Finishing off

When the time arrives for the concluding session, children will be at different stages of their work. Some will have finished, but many will still have work to do. The following strategies are recommended for dealing with this situation:
■ Expect children to be *on task* during the time allocated for writing.
■ Encourage them to work at a reasonable pace.
■ Make expectations of each group clear: 'I expect you to write at least a side during the next 20 minutes' (Groups 2 & 3). 'I want one paragraph of four or five lines written very carefully and checked over by the end of this session' (Group 4).
■ Give frequent time warnings such as 'We will have to stop writing in ten minutes'.
■ For key pieces of writing plan either a) homework to finish them off, or b) another hour of careful redrafting and presenting.
■ Discourage time-wasting activities such as decorating margins. Pictures should only be encouraged when they have a specific part to play (as in many non-fiction writing activities).

PHOTOCOPYING

Please note:
■ Where there is instruction to copy material from copyright texts, *you need to ensure that this is done within the limits of the copying licence your school has.*
■ If pupils are using their own exercise books or paper for answers, then all photocopiable resources are reuseable.

USE OF OVERHEAD PROJECTOR

Having the use of an overhead projector (OHP) is ideal for whole-class work. Photocopiable texts and skills activities can then be copied onto acetate to make overhead transparencies (OHTs) which can be projected onto a screen or a bare, white or light-coloured wall. For best effect, try to clear a whole section of wall from floor to ceiling and have it painted white. A partial black out would be an advantage. You will then be able to project a huge impressive text or picture. It can also be used to project backgrounds for drama improvisations. Where an OHP is not available, photocopiable sheets should be enlarged to at least A3 size.

INFORMATION AND COMPUTER TECHNOLOGY

Word processors have revolutionized the way we write, making redrafting less of a chore, and allowing documents to be well presented. However, the benefits of word processing only begin to be felt when the user has acquired a reasonable typing speed. It is therefore recommended that all children should use both hands on the keyboard and spend enough time practising so that they do not have to search for letters. To achieve this, word processing should be 'on the go' at all times. In most classrooms this will mean that a rota will have to be set up. When children have mastered the basics of word processing, they should be encouraged to make judgements about choice of fonts and page layout. The 'Words in Windows' and 'Writing Simulation' units provide good opportunities for this.

ASSESSMENT

Regular and ongoing assessment of children's achievements and progress is, of course, essential. These materials assume that you and your school have satisfactory methods and systems of assessing and recording already in place and therefore don't attempt to suggest an alternative. However, what these materials also assume is that your current procedures are based on clearly stated teaching objectives. Therefore the objectives grids at the beginning of each unit should be invaluable in providing you with a framework for ongoing assessment.

In addition, to facilitate individual children conferencing at the end of each half-term, a photocopiable record sheet has been provided on page 15. Specific targets for reading and writing can be set for each pupil at the end of the previous half-term and recorded on the sheet in the left-hand column. Interim progress towards these targets can be assessed when appropriate and noted in the middle column. Then, at the end of each half-term, during the conference, pupil and teacher together can record achievement and agree further targets for the next half-term.

HOMEWORK

The amount of homework should be increased throughout the Key Stage. In Year 3, it should be restricted to two types:

■ Finishing off work that could not be finished in class. *Note:* be careful how you manage this. Less able pupils are often the slowest workers, and could end up with the most homework. If there seems to be a lot of finishing off needed in children's own time, consider revising lesson plans to allow more time in school.

■ Preparation – for example finding texts, such as cereal packets, newspapers and so on, to be used in the next day's lesson.

PUPIL ASSESSMENT GRID

Pupil's name:				Class		Year group
Term	1	2	3	1st half		2nd half

	TARGET(S)	INTERIM PROGRESS (inc dates)	ACHIEVEMENT AT END OF HALF TERM
Reading			
Writing			

OVERVIEW: YEAR 3
TERM 1

	UNIT	SPELLING/ VOCABULARY	GRAMMAR/ PUNCTUATION	COMPREHENSION/ COMPOSITION
HOUR 5 (+5)	READING FICTION Modern fiction with familiar setting and sequel: *Dustbin Charlie* by Ann Pilling.	Know *i* before *e* spelling rule. Extend vocabulary from words in the text.	Recognize and use adjectives. Recognize and use nouns. Use capital letters for beginnings of sentences, names, places, days and months.	Develop basic reading skills. Identify setting. Identify and describe characters. Understand and discuss plot, and understand the term 'sequel'.
HOUR 5	WRITING FICTION Guided writing: 'Beat the Bully'.	Know -*y*/-*ies* plurals spelling rule. Extend vocabulary from text.	Recognize paragraphs. Indent paragraphs. Start a new paragraph for a new topic. Use of adjectives. Punctuation of speech.	Recall of simple facts, inference and deduction. Guided writing of a story with a simple structure, including dialogue. Build paragraphs with simple sentence patterns.
HOUR 2	READING NON-FICTION Recount (diary): Extract from *Swimming with Sea Lions* by Ann McGovern.	Extend vocabulary from vocabulary in text.	Know the term 'verb'. Recognize past and present verb tenses. Understand 1st and 3rd person and match verbs accordingly.	Develop basic reading skills. Practise skimming and scanning. Understand features of recount genre as used in diaries.
HOUR 1 (+1)	WRITING NON-FICTION Recount (diary): Extract from *Searching for Laura Ingalls* by Kathryn Lasky and Meribah Knight.	Spell and punctuate contractions.	Diary style: personal expression, first-person recount.	Write first-person recount: diary.
HOUR 1	REFERENCE AND RESEARCH Using a thesaurus.	Understand the meaning of the words 'thesaurus' and 'synonym'.	Understand what a synonym is. Investigate how the changing of words in a sentence has an impact on meaning.	Understand the purpose and organization of a thesaurus. Make use of a thesaurus to find synonyms.
HOUR 2	READING POETRY Classic Poem: 'The Months of the Year' by Sara Coleridge.	Recognize one- and two-syllable rhymes. Spell the months of the year.	Use grammatical knowledge to reassemble text. Revise adjectives.	Identify couplets. Demonstrate comprehension by resequencing.
HOUR 1 (+1)	WRITING POETRY Acrostic poems.	Understand alphabetical order.	Understand that the unit of poetry is the line and that poetry does not have to rhyme (free verse).	Write short, free-verse poems to the pattern provided by an acrostic.

NB **HOUR** 5 (+2) = Number of hours in unit (plus number of follow-up hours)

OVERVIEW: YEAR 3
TERM 1 (CONTINUED)

UNIT	SPELLING/ VOCABULARY	GRAMMAR/ PUNCTUATION	COMPREHENSION/ COMPOSITION
READING PLAYS 'Remote Control Kid'.	Understand and use vocabulary related to drama conventions.	Mark up a text to support reading aloud. Identify statements, questions, orders and exclamations.	Read a playscript with expression. Respond imaginatively to character and plot. Make simple notes.
WRITING PLAYS 'Little Red Riding Hood, 2000'.	Spell common words which include the letter combinations *ph* and *ck*.	Recognize the difference between standard and non-standard English.	Write a playscript using layout conventions correctly. Write convincing dialogue.
READING NON-FICTION Report genre: Weather Forecast.	Develop and understand vocabulary relating to weather.	Introduce the simple future tense.	Read and understand a weather map and report. Compare the way that the information is presented. Put the forecast into writing following simple model.
WRITING NON-FICTION Report genre: Weather Report.	Use vocabulary appropriate to weather description.	Revise the simple future tense.	Plan and present a weather report.
REFERENCE AND RESEARCH SKILLS Fact or Fiction?	Develop vocabulary related to library use and organization.		Distinguish between fact and fiction and understand the difference. Know how and where to find fiction and non-fiction books in the school library.
WORD PLAY Shape poems.	Explore vocabulary related to poem's topic.	Investigate the impact of layout on meaning.	Explore shape poems.

 NB 5 (+2) = Number of hours in unit (plus number of follow-up hours)

OVERVIEW: YEAR 3
TERM 2

UNIT	SPELLING/ VOCABULARY	GRAMMAR/ PUNCTUATION	COMPREHENSION/ COMPOSITION
READING FICTION Myths and legends: 'Pandora's Box'.	Spell -f/ves plurals. Pronunciation of Greek names by syllables. Vocabulary in text.	Revision and reinforcement of previously taught skills, including capital letters, nouns, verbs etc. Understand differences between verbs in the 1st and 3rd person and relate to different text types.	Develop basic reading skills. Develop skills of prediction, inference and deduction. Write portrait of story character in form of letter.
WRITING FICTION Writing myths using stimulus story cards: Myth-makers.	Break down long words into syllables. Use synonyms of 'said'.	Revise and extend writing of dialogue.	Apply story writing skills learned in 'Pandora's Box' unit, but with more imaginative content. Use a planning grid.
REDRAFTING SIMULATION 'Jason and the Golden Lyre'.	Identify misspelled words in own and others' writing.	Revise and consolidate grammar and punctuation skills.	Learn skills of redrafting through a simulation.
READING NON-FICTION Persuasion: Book Token.	Develop vocabulary from reading.	Revise present and past tenses. Understand person/verb agreement.	Develop basic reading skills. Identify and understand features of persuasive writing.
WRITING NON-FICTION Persuasion: Rules Rule!	Explore Greek and Latin prefixes.	Revise the imperative verb form.	Write a set of rules. Justify the rules.
REFERENCE AND RESEARCH SKILLS Alphabetical order.	Learn vocabulary for common reference books. Understand how dictionaries and thesauri can help with developing vocabulary.		Understand the purpose of alphabetical order. Practise using alphabetical order.
READING POETRY Cultural Variety: 'Song of the Animal Word' – a traditional Pygmy song.	Explore words that imitate sounds. Look at words with silent letters.	Mark up a text for reading aloud with intonation and expression.	Respond orally to a Pygmy song. Understand how layout aids meaning.
WRITING POETRY 'Animal Alphabet' by Zoe Goodall.	Know alphabetical order. Revise vowels and consonants.	Know when to use capital letters.	Use the alphabet as a pattern for writing a free-verse poem. Understand the term 'alliteration' and use the device in writing.

Hours per unit (shown in left margin): 3(+1), 3(+1), 2, 2, 2, 1, 2, 2

NB 5 (+2) = Number of hours in unit (plus number of follow-up hours)

OVERVIEW: YEAR 3
TERM 2 (CONTINUED)

UNIT	SPELLING/ VOCABULARY	GRAMMAR/ PUNCTUATION	COMPREHENSION/ COMPOSITION
READING NON-FICTION Procedural genre: How to Make a Paper Aeroplane.	Read, understand and spell appropriate language for subject matter. Understand abbreviations.	Use and understand the imperative verb form. Understand the need for concise writing.	Read and understand instructions.
READING NON-FICTION Procedural Genre: Party Time!	Spell words by syllables. Use and spell correctly appropriate vocabulary for procedural writing.	Use imperative verb form.	Write clear instructions for a variety of purposes. Use features of procedural genre.
READING NON-FICTION Packaging: 'Breakfast Bites'.	Explore opposites. Recognize how the suffixes -ful and -less influence word meaning.	Investigate the grammar of media text and slogans. Explore the use of capital letters in media texts. Identify essential words in sentences. Identify adjectives.	Read and discuss media texts. Explore ways of conveying ideas in a shortened form. Compare and contrast similar idea.
WRITING NON-FICTION Packaging: Cereal packet.	Identify different ways of spelling the same sound 'sh', 'ee'.	Experiment with deleting and substituting adjectives and noting the effect on meaning. Use capital letters for different purposes. Explore how appropriate fonts help to convey meaning.	Explore ways of writing ideas and messages, in shortened forms for media texts.
REFERENCE AND RESEARCH Making notes.	Understand the terms 'main idea' and 'key word'.	Identify key words and phrases which are essential to meaning.	Understand the purpose of note-making. Practise note-making.
WORD PLAY Rewriting nursery rhymes.	Identify rhyme families and note that the same sounds can be spelled in different ways.	Investigate punctuation and determine appropriate punctuation for own poem.	Understand that nursery rhymes are part of the oral tradition. Investigate rhyme patterns and rhymes in nursery rhymes.

HOUR 1(+1)

HOUR 2

HOUR 2

HOUR 2

HOUR 1

HOUR 1

NB 5 (+2) = Number of hours in unit (plus number of follow-up hours)

OVERVIEW: YEAR 3
TERM 3

UNIT	SPELLING/ VOCABULARY	GRAMMAR/ PUNCTUATION	COMPREHENSION/ COMPOSITION
HOUR 1 READING POETRY 'I'm Only Sleeping' by John Lennon and Paul McCartney.	Spell words with -ed, -ing, -able suffixes.	Identify nouns and verbs.	Respond to poem by comparing with own experiences. Revise rhyme and couplets.
HOUR 1 WRITING POETRY Clerihews.	Investigate phonics through rhyme.	Revise using capital letters for new lines of poetry.	Use rhyme effectively in the simplest rhyming form: the clerihew.
HOUR 5(+5) READING FICTION AND POETRY Short stories: *A Necklace of Raindrops* by Joan Aiken.	Investigate *igh*, *-ie* and *-y* rhyming words. Develop vocabulary from reading.	Introduce the term 'simile'. Explore adjectives for colour. Compare adjectives.	Identify themes. Discuss and map out plots. Distinguish fact *versus* fiction. Appreciate the figurative use of language. Compare and contrast stories.
HOUR 3 WRITING FICTION Write a story with a defined ending based on a proverb.	Identify misspelled words in own writing. Develop vocabulary from reading.	Understand the figurative use of words. Use the Redrafting Checklist as a basis for revision of key writing skills. Understand the figurative	nature of proverbs. Write stories which end with a proverb.
HOUR 4 READING NON-FICTION Information genre: *The Seashore* by Jane Walker.	Revise the terms 'heading', 'illustration' and 'caption'. Learn the terms 'subheading', 'font' and 'double-page spread'. Glossary Exercise on difficult words and terms in the text.	Use of present tense in information genre.	Reading information genre: understanding and using reference aids, eg contents, index and glossary. Understand how page design is used to present information clearly.
HOUR 2 WRITING NON-FICTION Explanation genre: Words in Windows.	Revise the terms 'heading', 'subheading', 'illustration', 'caption', 'font'. Introduce the term 'body text'.		Present information and explanations in the style of modern reference books.

NB **5 (+2)** = Number of hours in unit (plus number of follow-up hours)

UNIT	SPELLING/ VOCABULARY	GRAMMAR/ PUNCTUATION	COMPREHENSION/ COMPOSITION
HOUR 1 REFERENCE AND RESEARCH SKILLS Dictionary work.	To know and use words and phrases related to dictionary parts: 'guide word', 'headword', 'pronunciation', 'accent', 'syllable', 'definition', 'part of speech', 'origin'.	To understand the layout of a dictionary entry.	To understand that some dictionaries provide further information about words.
HOUR 5 READING FICTION Long-established fiction (Adventure): *Robin Hood and the Sheriff* by Julian Atterton.	Develop vocabulary from text, particularly archaic words and phrases.	Pronouns. Revision of parts of speech: nouns, pronouns, adjectives, verbs.	Study plot, character, language and ideas. Develop literal and inferential comprehension. Write a book review.
HOUR 4 WRITING FICTION Write a story in chapters: 'Pirate adventures'.	Identify misspelled words in own writing. Use synonyms for said and other high-frequency words.	Revise and consolidate key skills learned throughout the year using the Redrafting Checklist as a guide.	Write an episodic story in chapters modelled on known stories.
HOUR 5 WRITING SIMULATION Writing a magazine.	Correct spelling in proofreading exercise.	Redraft writing with attention to grammar and punctuation.	Recognize the distinctive features of magazines for young people and write own magazine. Explore letter-writing conventions. Revise skills for article, story and story writing.
HOUR 1 REFERENCE AND RESEARCH SKILLS Library classification system.	Develop vocabulary related to library usage.	To understand and use a classification code.	To understand library classification systems and use to locate books.
HOUR 1 WORD PLAY 'Conversation at the school dinner table' by John Rice.	Read nonsense words by phonic knowledge and by breaking down into syllables.	Investigate a humorous, alternative way of depicting speech.	Explore humour through word play.

NB **5 (+ 2)** = Number of hours in unit (plus number of follow-up hours)

OBJECTIVES GRIDS:
BLANK TEMPLATES

Use these blank photocopiable grids when inserting your own material.

UNIT	SPELLING/ VOCABULARY	GRAMMAR/ PUNCTUATION	COMPREHENSION/ COMPOSITION

UNIT	SPELLING/ VOCABULARY	GRAMMAR/ PUNCTUATION	COMPREHENSION/ COMPOSITION

UNIT	SPELLING/ VOCABULARY	GRAMMAR/ PUNCTUATION	COMPREHENSION/ COMPOSITION

UNIT	SPELLING/ VOCABULARY	GRAMMAR/ PUNCTUATION	COMPREHENSION/ COMPOSITION

Term 1

DUSTBIN CHARLIE

OBJECTIVES

UNIT	SPELLING/VOCABULARY	GRAMMAR/PUNCTUATION	COMPREHENSION/ COMPOSITION
READING FICTION Modern fiction with familiar setting and sequel: *Dustbin Charlie* by Ann Pilling.	Know *i before e* spelling rule. Extend vocabulary from words in the text.	Recognize and use adjectives. Recognize and use nouns. Use capital letters for beginnings of sentences, names, places, days and months.	Develop basic reading skills. Identify setting. Identify and describe characters. Understand and discuss plot, and understand the term 'sequel'.

ORGANIZATION (5 HOURS)

	INTRODUCTION	WHOLE-CLASS SKILLS WORK	DIFFERENTIATED GROUP ACTIVITIES	CONCLUSION
HOUR 1	Shared reading from beginning to page 19, establishing setting and characters.	Exercise on adjectives.	1*: Guided reading to page 19 followed by discussion with teacher. 2 & 3: Write character descriptions of Charlie and Grandad. 4*: Guided reading to page 19, followed by discussion, all with teacher.	Share selected character descriptions and sum up story so far.
HOUR 2	Read pages 20 to 34.	Exercise on nouns.	1: Discuss what might be in the skip. Make list. Add adjectives to list. 2 & 3*: Guided reading of pages 20 to 34 followed by discussion with teacher. 4: Discuss what might be in the skip. Make list.	Read to middle of page 42 to find out what has actually been put into skip.
HOUR 3	Read pages 42 to 55.	Exercise on capital letters (names and places).	1*: Guided reading of pages 42 to 55 followed by discussion with teacher. 2 & 3: Study use of capital letters in story. 4*: Guided reading of pages 42 to 55 with teacher followed by discussion.	Groups 2 & 3 present their work using OHP and appropriate coloured pens if available.
HOUR 4	Read pages 56 to 77.	Teach *i before e* spelling rule.	1: Write character descriptions of Grandma and Curly Harry. 2 & 3*: Guided reading of pages 56 to 77 followed by discussion with teacher. 4: Study use of capital letters in story.	Share selected character descriptions and sum up story so far.
HOUR 5	Read pages 78 to end.	Explain the term 'sequel'.	1–4*: Write another adventure for Dustbin Charlie and the Tin Man.	Selected pupils read out their adventures. Class evaluates how effective they are as sequels.

RESOURCES

Dustbin Charlie by Ann Pilling (Young Puffin, ISBN 0-14-032391-0) – if possible, enough copies for half the class, photocopiable pages 28 (Adjectives), 29 (Nouns), 30 (Capital Letters), 31 (Union Street Characters) and 32 (Useful Character Adjectives), board or flip chart, OHP and acetate (optional), coloured pens, writing materials.

PREPARATION

If possible, make two OHTs, one of the text on pages 7–9 of *Dustbin Charlie* and one of the text on pages 20–21. If this is not possible, make copies enlarged to A3 size. Make enough copies of photocopiable pages 28 (Adjectives), 29 (Nouns) and 30 (Capital Letters) for one between two, and enough copies of pages 31 (Union Street Characters) and 32 (Useful Character Adjectives) for one each.

SYNOPSIS

Charlie lives on a farm, but finds it far more exciting to visit his grandparents in the city. He particularly likes to see what people have thrown away in their dustbins. One day a skip is delivered to the house across the street and the neighbours quickly fill it with their rubbish. Charlie is thrilled to discover in it the toy he has always wanted. But during the night, the toy disappears from the skip. Charlie is devastated. Who has taken it? It turns out to be Grandad, who has secretly cleaned it up and mended it.

Introduction

Introduce the book by reading the blurb on page 1. Then read from the beginning of the story to page 9. If you are able to display an OHT or enlarged photocopy of the text, then do so and discuss where the story is set. In fact, two contrasting settings are described, and these set up the reason for Charlie's visit to his grandad's house. Continue reading to page 19.

Whole-class skills work

Teach or review the term 'adjective'. Explain that an adjective is a describing word. Give out copies of photocopiable page 28 (Adjectives), one between two. Look at the examples in the first box on the sheet and ask the class to brainstorm more adjectives for the given examples. Then do the exercise. This emphasizes the importance of *choosing* the best adjective for the job. Discuss choices for each one. The second part is more open-ended, with children thinking of their own adjectives. Less able children may need support here.

Differentiated group activities

1*: Re-read the book to page 19 and discuss it (with the teacher or an adult helper) using these questions as a starting point. Encourage the children to support their responses by referring to the story and the pictures.
■ Do you remember what Dustbin Charlie's real name was?
■ Why did he like dustbins so much?
■ What did his grandad like doing?
■ What was he mending?
■ What sort of a boy is Charlie? Does he look happy?
■ What is his grandad like? Does he look kind?
2 & 3: Write character descriptions of Charlie and Grandad on the Union Street Characters photocopiable sheet (page 31), using evidence from both text and pictures. Begin by thinking of two adjectives to describe each character (the Useful Character Adjectives photocopiable sheet on page 32 may be helpful for this). Then use the chosen adjectives in their description, underlining them and other adjectives.
4*: Re-read with the teacher and discuss the passage as described above. Take particular care to monitor basic reading skills as the children re-read the passage.

Conclusion

Share some of the character descriptions written by children in Groups 2 and 3 and discuss the appropriateness of the adjectives they chose. To round off the hour, sum up the story so far, to leave children with a clear sense of where they are in the story.

Introduction

Read from page 20 to 34.

Whole-class skills work

Give out copies of photocopiable page 29 (Nouns), one between two. Teach or revise the term 'noun'. Ask if any children know/remember what a noun is. Then read the definition on the sheet to confirm the definition. Teach or revise the use of capital letters for nouns which are the names of people and places. Then ask the children to complete the columns with their own examples, and discuss.

Differentiated group activities

1: Ask the children to fold a sheet of paper in half to make two columns. Tell them to head the first column ADJECTIVES and the second, NOUNS. They should discuss what might be in the skip and make a list in the *second* column. They should then, in the first column, write an adjective for each noun they have listed.

2 & 3*: Re-read pages 20 to 34 and discuss with the teacher what might be in the skip. The teacher should make the point that these items are nouns. Discuss appropriate adjectives to describe these nouns.

4: Write the title NOUNS on a sheet of paper, and make a list of the things that might be in the skip.

Conclusion

Read to the middle of page 42 (ending with 'She sounded a bit mad.') to find out what has actually been put into the skip. Discuss the accuracy of the predictions of children in Groups 2 and 3.

Introduction

Recap on the story so far. Read pages 42 to 55. Discuss briefly the humour involved when Grandma doesn't hear Charlie properly. The author is having some fun with words that rhyme.

Whole-class skills work

Use photocopiable page 30 (Capital Letters) (one copy between two) to teach or revise the use of capital letters – in particular for beginning sentences, names and places, days, months and special occasions.

Differentiated group activities

1*: Re-read pages 42 to 55. Discuss with the teacher, using the following questions as a starting point:
■ What things are missing from the skip?
■ What do you think happened to them?

2 & 3: On a copy of pages 20–21, underline each capital letter using a colour code for different uses, such as red to start a sentence; green for a place name; blue for a person's name. Two colours will be needed for some letters!

4*: Re-read pages 42 to 55 with the teacher and discuss the section as above. The teacher should give particular attention to basic reading skills.

Conclusion

Groups 2 and 3 present their work to the rest of the class using an OHP and appropriate coloured pens if available. If an OHP is not available, enlarge the pages to A3 size and use them as a poster.

Introduction

Recap on the story so far and, using suggestions from the group work of the previous hour, discuss what might have happened to the missing items. Suggestions could be listed on the board or flip chart for future reference. Read pages 56 to 77.

Whole-class skills work

Use Charlie's name to introduce the spelling rule: 'Write *i* before *e* except after *c* when the sound is ee'. Write the rule on the board or flip chart with examples as shown.

RULE: Write *i* before e except after c when the sound is ee.
- Examples of 'i before e' words: *believe*, *thief.*
- Examples of 'e before i' words: c*eiling, receive.*
- Examples of exceptions to the rule: *seize, weird.*

Make sure the children learn the rule and the exceptions by heart. Now write up a grid like the one below and work with the class to fill in more examples:

i before e words	e before i words	exceptions
believe	ceiling	seize
thief	receive	weird

(Other 'i before e' words: *achieve, brief, chief, field, grief, piece, shield, siege*; 'e before i' words: *deceive, conceit, perceive*; exceptions: *neither, weir.*)

Differentiated group activities

1: Write character descriptions of Grandma and Curly Harry on photocopiable page 31 (Union Street Characters), as Groups 2 and 3 did for Charlie and Grandad in Hour 1.
2 & 3*: Re-read pages 56–77 followed by discussion with the teacher. Use these questions as starting points:
- In your own words, describe Curly Harry.
- What do you think he lives on?
- How do you think he came to be a tramp?
- Think of two adjectives to describe him.
4: As for Groups 2 and 3 in Hour 3. The fact that they have seen this presented by another group the day before will support their work.

Conclusion

Share some of the descriptions of Grandma and Curly Harry. Sum up the story so far and ask for ideas about who they think took the Tin Man.

Introduction

Read pages 78 to the end. Discuss if they were able to guess correctly who took the Tin Man. What clues in the story might have helped them?

Whole-class skills work

Explain the term 'sequel'. Usually a sequel has some of the same main characters and the same setting. Recap the main characters and setting of *Dustbin Charlie.* Do they know of any other stories in books or on TV that are set in a street or neighborhood and have the same characters in different stories? Tell the class that Ann Pilling has written a sequel to *Dustbin Charlie* called *Dustbin Charlie Cleans Up.* (If you are going to use the Follow-up unit on it (see below), tell the children. Otherwise suggest they read it for themselves.) Explain that they are now going to write their own sequel.

Differentiated group activities

1–4*: All children write another adventure for Dustbin Charlie and the Tin Man. The teacher gives support where needed.

Conclusion

Selected children read out their adventures. The class evaluate how effective each one is as a sequel: Did it use the same characters? Did the characters act and talk in the same way? Was it set in the same place?

FOLLOW-UP (5 HOURS)

See page 202 which provides a grid plan for a 5-hour follow-up unit on the sequel to *Dustbin Charlie (Dustbin Charlie Cleans Up* by Ann Pilling, Young Puffin ISBN 0-14-036406-4).

ADJECTIVES

An adjective is a describing word. Here are some examples:
- Charlie liked watching the **rubbish** men with their **yellow** lorry.
- Charlie held the **silver** plate.
- We don't have **smelly** dustbins any more.
- We have **shiny black** bags.

■ Read the passage below. Each time you reach three adjectives in brackets choose the one you want to use by underlining it. Finish off by filling the gaps with your own adjectives.

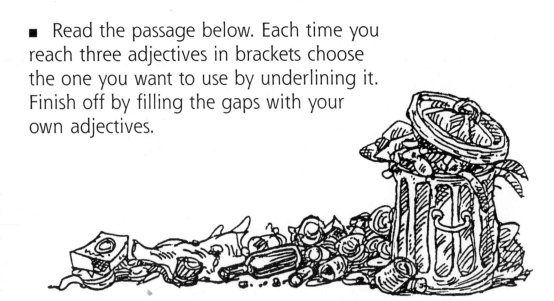

In our town, Monday is rubbish day. The dustmen come in a (green, rusty, smelly) lorry. They wear (dirty, clean, blue) overalls and (thick, large, heavy) gloves. Our bin is made of (pink, yellow, black) plastic and it has two (tiny, huge, round) wheels.

I have a _____ waste bin in my bedroom. It is full of _____ paper, _____ toys and _____ rubbish. Ooops! I forgot to empty it! Now, it's a whole week until next Monday.

NOUNS

A noun is a naming word.
Nouns are used to name people, places or things.

■ Add more nouns to each column. If it is the name of a person or place it should begin with a capital letter like 'Charlie' and 'Union Street'.

PEOPLE	PLACES	THINGS
Charlie	Union Street	lorry
Grandad	farmyard	dustbin
baby	garden	sheep
tramp	town	bottle

THIS WAY TO UNION STREET

CAPITAL LETTERS

RULE: Capital letters are used for:

BEGINNING SENTENCES: His real name was 'Timothy Charles Treadwell'.

NAMES: Charlie, Curly Harry, Mrs Bats

PLACES: Union Street, London, America

DAYS, MONTHS, SPECIAL OCCASIONS: Tuesday, January, Christmas

■ Rewrite this paragraph using capital letters where needed:

It was a wet and windy monday morning in the month of february. in the whole town of clifton, only two people were out. sally smith was on her way to buy a valentine's day card and mrs murphy was just putting her dustbin out. suddenly the wind caught her bin and blew it over. litter from the bin swept down wordsworth street. sally had just opened her mouth to laugh when a newspaper from mrs murphy's bin covered her whole head!

UNION STREET CHARACTERS

■ Underneath each picture write about the character. Use the words and pictures from the book to help you. First, think of two adjectives to describe each character. Then write a description using the two adjectives you have chosen. Underline these adjectives and any others that you use.

Adjectives

Description

Adjectives

Description

Adjectives

Description

Adjectives

Description

USEFUL CHARACTER ADJECTIVES

adventurous	grumpy	scruffy
aggressive	handsome	short
beautiful	happy	shy
bold	hard-working	silly
boring	helpful	slim
calm	honest	smart
caring	merry	spotty
clever	moody	stupid
	neat	sweet
	plain	tall
cunning	plump	ugly
cute	practical	wrinkled
dainty	pretty	
funny	rich	
good-looking	rough	

BEAT THE BULLY

OBJECTIVES

UNIT	SPELLING/VOCABULARY	GRAMMAR/PUNCTUATION	COMPREHENSION/ COMPOSITION
WRITING FICTION Guided writing: 'Beat the Bully'.	Know -y/-ies plurals spelling rule. Extend vocabulary from text.	Recognize paragraphs. Indent paragraphs. Start a new paragraph for a new topic. Use of adjectives. Punctuation of speech.	Recall of simple facts, inference and deduction. Guided writing of a story with a simple structure, including dialogue. Build paragraphs with simple sentence patterns.

ORGANIZATION (5 HOURS)

	INTRODUCTION	WHOLE-CLASS SKILLS WORK	DIFFERENTIATED GROUP ACTIVITIES	CONCLUSION
HOUR 1	Read 'Beat the Bully'. Explain story structure. Read opening paragraphs again and discuss use of adjectives.	Paragraphs: explain how they are set out.	1*: Guided writing using text as a model. 2 & 3: Reading Comprehension – parts A, B & C. 4*: Guided writing.	Selected pupils from Groups 1 & 4 share their story beginnings, followed by brief discussion.
HOUR 2	Re-read 'Beat the Bully', focusing on the sections with dialogue.	Dialogue: explain its punctuation, emphasizing use of speech marks. Short exercise on speech marks.	1: Reading Comprehension – parts A, B & C. 2 & 3*: Guided writing. 4: Reading Comprehension – parts A, B & C.	Selected pupils from Groups 2 & 3 share their story beginnings, followed by brief discussion.
HOUR 3	Re-read the first bullying incident. Discuss the development (the middle) of the story.	Revise the terms 'singular' and 'plural' using part A of the photocopiable sheet.	1*: Writing (continued). 2 & 3: Reading Comprehension – parts D & E. 4* Writing (continued).	Selected pupils from Groups 2 & 3 give a presentation of the text and share some comprehension answers.
HOUR 4	Re-read the ending of 'Beat the Bully' and discuss different ways of ending a bullying story.	Teach the rule for -y/-ies plurals using part B of the photocopiable sheet.	1: Reading Comprehension – parts D & E. 2 & 3*: Writing (continued). 4: Reading Comprehension – parts C & E.	Selected pupils from Groups 1 & 4 give a presentation of the text and share some comprehension answers.
HOUR 5	Recap on the main points of the story and explain the story structure.	Redrafting: explain what to look for.	1–4*: Redrafting and finishing off.	Selected pupils read out stories followed by evaluation.

RESOURCES

Photocopiable pages 37 ('Beat the Bully'), 38 (Character Sheet), 39 (Story Template), 40 (Reading Comprehension), 41 (Punctuating Speech), 42 (Singular and Plural), and 32 (Useful Character Adjectives from 'Dustbin Charlie' unit), board or flip chart, OHP and acetate (optional), lined paper with ruled margins, writing materials.

Preparation

A set of all photocopiable resources should be prepared for each pair of children. It is useful, in addition, to make OHTs of the story and the Character Sheet as a focus for whole-class discussion.

It is recommended that children should write on lined paper with a ruled margin as this helps with indentation and clear paragraph layout.

Introduction

Read 'Beat the Bully' on page 37. Explain how the story structure works and write it out on the board as follows:

Beginning: Description of the main character and the second character.
Middle: Narration of the main incident.
End: A solution to the problem.

Discuss with the children to ensure that they can see how 'Beat the Bully' fits this structure. Re-read the opening paragraphs again and discuss the way in which adjectives are used to describe the characters.

Whole-class skills work

Explain paragraphing conventions with reference to the story and teach the terms 'indent' and 'indentation'. Explain to the children that except for the first paragraph (which is not usually indented), they should indent the first line of a paragraph approximately 1cm, or a 'finger space'. No blank lines should be left between paragraphs. Ask children to find the paragraph divisions in the story and to look for the indentations. More able children should be asked to note the indentation and layout of dialogue.

Differentiated group activities

1 & 4*: Start both groups together by looking at the characters on photocopiable page 38 (Character Sheet). Discuss which characters might be good and which might be bullies. Raise the issue of stereotypes and characters with contradictory images (perhaps scruffy looks, but a warm smile). Can you tell a bully by the way he/she looks? Ask children (individually or in pairs) to choose a 'good' character and a bully and to give each a name. They should write the names on the sheet, then write two adjectives for each character (they could use the Useful Character Adjectives sheet on page 32 to help them if they wish). Group 4 should then use the filled-in sheet to begin writing directly onto the Story Template (page 39). Explain that blanks with a line are for names, and blanks with dots are for other words.

The first paragraph begins with the name of the good character in the story. The second blank requires an appropriate adjective, as does the third blank in paragraph 2. Other blanks can be completed in any way that makes sense.

More able children in Group 4 should be encouraged to add extra sentences in the space between paragraphs. Group 1 children should be encouraged to write with more freedom, but to use the 'Beat the Bully' story and Story Template sheet as models for structure, use of adjectives, paragraphs, speech marks and so on.

2 & 3: Children in these groups work on parts A, B and C of the Reading Comprehension sheet on page 40.

Conclusion

Choose selected children from Groups 1 and 4 to read out their story beginnings. Discuss briefly some of the successful aspects.

Introduction

Re-read the sections of the story with dialogue, perhaps dividing the class in half to take the two parts. Explain how dialogue is punctuated and set out. Point out the two main things that they need to learn:
- to use speech marks before and after words actually spoken
- to place a comma, full stop, question mark or exclamation mark before the final speech marks.

Whole-class skills work

Use photocopiable page 41 (Punctuating Speech) to teach the conventions of speech marks and punctuation in dialogue. You could work through the whole sheet with the class or, after modelling a couple of examples in parts A and B, let children complete the sheet themselves.

Group 4, and less able children from Groups 2 and 3, should concentrate on part A. Others from Groups 2 and 3 should concentrate on part B. Group 1 should do part B, and those who complete this accurately could be asked to write a short dialogue, concentrating on setting it out correctly, writing a new, indented line for every change of speaker.

Differentiated group activities

1: Work on parts A, B and C of the Reading Comprehension sheet (page 40).
2 & 3*: Write the story as described in Hour 1, but using the template as a guide. In other words, they should follow it closely, but can expand sentences and add extra description. Encourage children to use some dialogue in the third paragraph.
4: Work on parts A and B of the Reading Comprehension sheet (page 40).

Conclusion

Selected children from Groups 2 and 3 read their story beginnings, followed by brief discussion as in Hour 1.

Introduction

Re-read the first bullying incident. Discuss the development (the middle) of the story. What should someone do when they have been bullied? What did Tim do? What could the characters in your stories do?

Whole-class skills work

Revise the terms 'singular' and 'plural'. Use part A of photocopiable page 42 (Singular and Plural) as a whole-class activity.

Differentiated group activities

1*: Continue writing their own 'Beat the Bully' story. Give support by discussing progress so far and suitable endings. Children in this group should aim at endings of about two or three paragraphs in length.
2 & 3: Work on parts D and E of the Reading Comprehension sheet (page 40) which invite open-ended discussion on the subject of bullying to explore the Personal, Moral, Social and Cultural Education aspects of the theme. Complete any outstanding work on parts A, B and C.
4*: Children in this group should now have finished, or nearly finished the third paragraph. Discuss suitable endings to the story and explain that their ending will be a fourth paragraph that they will write on their own.

Conclusion

Selected children from Groups 2 and 3 give a presentation of the text and share some of their responses to the Reading Comprehension sheet.

Introduction

Re-read the ending of 'Beat the Bully'. Ask the children if they liked the ending of the story and to give reasons for their answers. Discuss different ways of concluding a bullying story (point out that humour is used in the text). Explain that the reader needs to feel satisfied that the main character has solved the problem and that the bully has been punished.

Whole-class skills work

Using part A of photocopiable page 42 (Singular and Plural), briefly revise s and es plurals. Then use part B to explain the rule about plurals of words ending in y, using examples from the story such as *bully*, *hobby* or *butterfly*. Encourage children to memorize the rule. More able children could be asked to brainstorm further examples of -*y*/-*ies* plurals.

Differentiated group activities

1: Work on parts D and E of the Reading Comprehension sheet (page 40). Complete any outstanding work on parts A, B and C.

2 & 3*: Continue their story as described above. Explain that they may need two or three more paragraphs to bring the story to a conclusion.

4. Work on parts C and E of the Reading Comprehension sheet (page 40).

Conclusion

Selected children from Groups 1 and 4 give a presentation of the text and share some of their responses to the Reading Comprehension sheet (page 40).

HOUR 5

Introduction

Remind children of the basic structure of 'Beat the Bully' and the stories that they have written. Ask them to copy down the chart written on the board in Hour 1, so that it can be used again as a structure for a story with different content.

Whole-class skills work

Give guidance on redrafting. Ask children to work with a partner in a two-stage process:
■ Stage 1: read through the story and look for places where the description can be made more detailed and improved.
■ Stage 2: proofread the story for spelling, grammar and punctuation mistakes. Look particularly for the skills covered during the week.

Differentiated group activities

1–4*: All four groups redraft their stories. The teacher should work briefly with all groups, but give particular attention to Group 4, and some of the weaker children in Groups 2 and 3. This is an opportunity for each child to rewrite his or her story and add more of his or her own ideas.

Conclusion

Selected children read out their complete story followed by evaluation by the whole class. Ask the class to comment on the following:
■ How closely did the story keep to the recommended structure?
■ Were the adjectives well chosen?
■ Was the dialogue true to life?
■ Was the ending satisfying?
■ How did it compare with the original story?

BEAT THE BULLY

Tim was a quiet boy who went to school at St Andrew's County Primary. His short, brown hair was spikey and his eyes were bright and intelligent. He liked to spend his spare time on his hobbies, which were watching the science channel on cable television and collecting insects. Above all, he liked butterflies. He would catch them in a special net so he could draw pictures of them. Then, with a whoosh, he would set them free into the air.

Unfortunately, Tim was bullied by Billy. Billy was a rough, clumsy boy who liked to hang around street corners eating junk food. He rarely turned up for school and, when he did, he usually got himself into trouble before morning break.

One day, Tim was walking home from school when Billy jumped out from behind a bush and pushed him over. Tim grazed his knee and, even worse, his homework got all muddy – which meant he would certainly get into trouble the next day. He felt hurt and upset, and had to choke back the tears as he picked himself up. Luckily, Billy was now nowhere to be seen. So Tim brushed himself down and hoped that his mum wouldn't notice – but, of course, she did!

'Just look at you!' she shouted when he walked in.

'Sorry!' said Tim, glancing down at his torn and muddy trousers.

'What on earth have you been doing?'

'Oh...er...nothing.' Tim hoped she wouldn't make a fuss.

'I bet you've been chasing those creepy crawlies again!'

'Er...sort of,' mumbled Tim. And that wasn't a lie, because Billy *was* a creepie crawlie!

Luckily his mum said no more on the subject, which was just as well as Tim felt that he was close to tears.

However, next morning something happened that really cheered Tim up. On the way to school he found the finest specimen of a big black beetle he had ever seen. It was bigger than a 50-pence piece! He picked it up, clutched it in the palm of his hand and hurried on to school so he could put it safely in a jam jar.

But then he saw Billy, waiting at the school gate. As usual he was teasing and bullying the children who passed, particularly the smallest ones.

'What have you got there?' he said, looking at Tim's clenched fist.

'Oh...er...nothing,' said Tim anxiously.

'It looks like money to me,' said Billy, '50 pence, I'll bet! Give it here!' He grabbed Tim's hand and prised it open.

Tim was totally amazed at what happened next. Billy froze to the spot and his face went white. At the same time he let out an ear-piercing scream. Then he started gibbering like a mad baboon.

'Aaarrrggghhh!!! A beetle! Don't let it touch me! Please, help! I'll do anything! Save me and you can have my crisps! Help!' All the children in the playground watched in astonishment as Billy handed over his bag of crisps and ran away sobbing.

From that day on there was no more bullying from Billy, but Tim always carried a big black beetle in his pocket – just in case!

CHARACTER SHEET

■ Discuss: Which of these characters do you think are 'good'? Which are 'bullies'?

■ Choose one 'good' character and one 'bully' character for your story. Give each character a name. Then think of at least two adjectives to describe each one.

Name: _____

Adjectives: _____

_____

Name: _____

Adjectives: _____

_____

Name: _____

Adjectives: _____

_____

Name: _____

Adjectives: _____

_____

Name: _____

Adjectives: _____

_____

Name: _____

Adjectives: _____

_____

STORY TEMPLATE

■ Use this sheet to help you with sentences and paragraphs. Do not write on the sheet unless your teacher tells you to.

_____ was a(n) .... person who went to school at .... His/her hair was .... and his/her eyes were .... He/she liked .... and ....

Unfortunately _____ was bullied by _____. _____ was a(n) .... and .... person who liked .... and ....

One day, when _____ was walking to school, _____ came up and.......................... ....

■ Finish the story by describing what the main character did to beat the bully.

READING COMPREHENSION

PART A

In your Word Book, write down the meaning of the words that are underlined. If you are not sure of the meaning, check in a dictionary.

1. Tim grazed his knee.
2. He found the finest specimen of a big black beetle he had ever seen.
3. 'Oh...er...nothing,' said Tim anxiously.
4. He grabbed Tim's hand and prised it open.
5. Then he started gibbering like a mad baboon.

PART B

In pairs or threes, prepare to read the 'Beat the Bully' text aloud to the class. You could prepare the text by:
■ looking up the meanings of any other words you are not sure about
■ going over all punctuation in red
■ underlining the words you need to emphasize
■ marking who reads each section.

PART C

In pairs, talk about these questions, then write your answers:
1. What were Tim's favourite hobbies?
2. How did Billy hurt Tim?
3. What did Billy think Tim was hiding?
4. Why was Billy so frightened?
5. Why did Tim always carry a beetle from that day on?

PART D

In pairs, talk about these questions, then write your answers:
1. What is it about Tim's character that might encourage other people to bully him?
2. How did Tim feel when he had been bullied?
3. Why did Tim hope his mother would not notice that he had been bullied?
4. Why do you think Billy was a bully?
5. Do you think that the ending of the story could happen in real life?

PART E

Discuss together:
Has someone you know (or seen on television perhaps) ever been bullied? How did it start? What happened? How did it end?

PUNCTUATING SPEECH

PART A

> **RULE:** Speech marks are placed before and after the words which are spoken:
>
> **"I like to collect butterflies," said Tim.**

Place speech marks before and after spoken words:

1. Give me your money Billy said.

2. What an interesting beetle said Tim.

3. I don't like creepy crawlies admitted Billy.

4. Tim said look at this.

5. Help screamed Billy.

6. How did that happen asked Mum.

PART B

> **RULE:** Before the final speech marks there is always a comma, exclamation mark or question mark – or a full stop if the sentence ends there.
>
> **Tim said, "Go away."**   **"What a huge spider!" gasped Billy.**
>
> **"Who's that?" asked Tim.**   **"Here is your tea," said Mum.**

Put in the speech marks and other punctuation.

1. Take that out of here at once exclaimed Mum

2. Where is my butterfly net asked Tim

3. Billy said I'll see you after school

4. This is my pet spider said Ann

5. Can I cuddle it asked Tim

6. Don't touch it shouted Dad

SINGULAR AND PLURAL

PART A

> **RULE:** The plural of most nouns is formed by adding s or es:
>
> | SINGULAR (one) | PLURAL (more than one) |
> |---|---|
> | spider | spiders |
> | sweet | sweets |
> | dish | dishes |

Copy out and complete this list:

SINGULAR (one)	PLURAL (more than one)
beetle	
insect	
bush	
puddle	
box	
corner	
chocolate	
piece	
hand	

PART B

> **RULE:** Words ending in y change the y to i and add es if the letter before y is a consonant.
>
> NOTE: If the rule does not apply, the word will *look* wrong – *railwaies*, for example:
>
> | SINGULAR (one) | PLURAL (more than one) |
> |---|---|
> | bully | bullies |
> | butterfly | butterflies |
> | story | stories |

Copy out and complete this list:

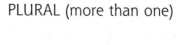

SINGULAR (one)	PLURAL (more than one)
hobby	
fly	
city	
toy	
baby	
lorry	
holiday	
dictionary	
tray	

SWIMMING WITH SEA LIONS

OBJECTIVES

UNIT	SPELLING/VOCABULARY	GRAMMAR/PUNCTUATION	COMPREHENSION/ COMPOSITION
READING NON-FICTION Recount (diary): Extract from *Swimming with Sea Lions* by Ann McGovern.	Extend vocabulary from vocabulary in text.	Know the term 'verb'. Recognize past and present verb tenses. Understand 1st and 3rd person and match verbs accordingly.	Develop basic reading skills. Practise skimming and scanning. Understand features of recount genre as used in diaries.

ORGANIZATION (2 HOURS)

	INTRODUCTION	WHOLE-CLASS SKILLS WORK	DIFFERENTIATED GROUP ACTIVITIES	CONCLUSION
HOUR 1	Briefly explain the background and read extract from *Swimming with Sea Lions*.	Exercise on verbs in the simple present and regular past tense. Demonstrate how to skim and scan the text to find answers to comprehension questions.	1 & 2: Start working through the Reading Comprehension sheet independently. 3*: Guided reading of the diary and discuss parts A and B of the Reading Comprehension sheet. 4*: As above, but part A only.	Discuss answers to part A of the Reading Comprehension sheet.
HOUR 2	Re-read extract. Ask pupils to listen for the word 'I' and expressions of personal thoughts and feelings.	Focus on the style of diary writing (first person recount) and make comparison with third person.	1 & 2*: Discuss the text and written answers to part B of the Reading Comprehension sheet with the teacher. Work on part C of the Reading Comprehension sheet. 3: Write answers for part A and as much of part B as possible. 4: Write answers for part A of the Reading Comprehension sheet.	Discuss answers to part B of the Reading Comprehension sheet. Give Group 4 (who have not done this section) simple explanations where appropriate.

RESOURCES

Photocopiable pages 45 and 46 ('Swimming with Sea Lions'), 47 (Verbs) and 48 (Reading Comprehension), board or flip chart, OHP and acetate (optional), world map, coloured pens or pencils, writing materials.

PREPARATION

Photocopy enough sets of the diary extracts (pages 45 and 46) and the Verbs sheet (page 47) for one between two (if possible, photocopy the diary extracts as a double-page spread on A3 paper). Ideally, children will need one Reading Comprehension sheet (page 48) each.

Write out the examples of verbs (see photocopiable page 47) for Hour 1 ('Whole-class skills work') on the board, chart or an OHT.

Introduction

Discuss briefly the background to the diary extract which is printed at the top of photocopiable page 45. Explain the literary term 'extract'. Locate the Galápagos Islands on a map and ensure that the children know the correct pronunciation (Ga-**láp**-a-gos). Then share the extract from Ann's diary.

Whole-class skills work

Give out photocopiable page 47 (Verbs), one between two. Ask children what they know about verbs, then consolidate and extend their knowledge by carefully explaining the definition and examples in the box. The verb conjugations ('conjugation' means writing out all the parts of the verb as in the example, but do not use this term with children at this level) will need careful explanation. Tell them that the chart simply shows a way of writing out the verb in all its forms. Ask children to make a similar chart for the other regular verbs listed on the sheet. More able children could go on to irregular verbs.

Before starting the Reading Comprehension sheet, demonstrate how to skim and scan the text to find answers to the questions.

Differentiated group activities

All groups work on the Reading Comprehension sheet (page 48).
1 & 2: Children work through parts A and B independently. Encourage them to work quickly through part A so that they can spend more time on part B.
3 & 4*: The teacher should spend time supporting Group 4 first. Help them to re-read the diary and talk them through the questions in part A, then leave them to find and discuss their answers in pairs. Move on to Group 3, who should have completed their re-reading of the diary by now, so the focus can be on helping them with the Reading Comprehension questions. Some of this group may be able to do part B with support.

Conclusion

Discuss answers to part A of the Reading Comprehension sheet. Ask children where they found the answers, and how long it took to find them. Reinforce the advantage of good skimming and scanning skills – they help us to find what we want to know more quickly.

Introduction

Re-read *Swimming with Sea Lions*. Ask children to listen for the words 'I', 'me' and 'my' and expressions of personal thoughts and feelings. (Children could even count the number of times the word 'I' is used!) Discuss the fact that the inclusion of personal feelings and responses is a characteristic of diary writing. Ask the children to find examples, such as *'I can't believe…'*, *'I'm so excited!'*, *'I am so mad I could cry!'*

Whole-class skills work

Focus on the style of diary writing (1st-person recount). Explain that diaries are written in the 1st person. To help children to understand this, refer them to the verbs they wrote out in Hour 1. They will also see that the 3rd person is 'He/she/it' ('they' in the plural). To illustrate the difference, try changing one of the paragraphs from the diary from 1st person into 3rd person, for example *'She can't believe that she and Grandma have already…'.* Ensure they see the difference between the personal voice and the 'narrative' voice.

Differentiated group activities

1 & 2:* Discuss the text and their written answers to the Reading Comprehension sheet, particularly part B, with the teacher. Work on part C can be set up as follow-up work for the library or after school.
3: Write answers for part A of the Reading Comprehension sheet and as much of part B as possible (where appropriate).
4: Write out answers for part A of the Reading Comprehension sheet and mark in the text of the diary where they found their answers.

Conclusion

Discuss answers to part B. Include Group 4 (who have not done this section) by giving simple explanations where appropriate. Emphasize particularly the last question which helps children to see the personal nature of diary writing.

SWIMMING WITH SEA LIONS

Ann McGovern's grandmother always dreamed of going to the Galápagos Islands, 600 miles west of the mainland of Equador, South America. It is a place that is rich with unusual wildlife and plants. When she finally got a chance to go, she invited Ann to go with her. While there, Ann kept a diary which was later published as a book. Here is an extract.

Day One
First day in the Galápagos!!!

Dear Diary,

I can't believe that Grandma and I have already spent almost a whole day in the Galápagos Islands. Everything is like a strange dream. Today I walked right up to birds and they didn't fly away! Grandma talked to sea lions – and they talked back with funny barks and burps. I've never seen such tame wild creatures in my whole life! Living on a boat is strange, too. Our boat is called the *Mistral*.

I think I'll start from the beginning. There was snow on the ground when Grandma and I left New York. After three different plane rides, we came to these hot islands on the equator, in the Pacific Ocean! When we landed at the little airport, we were met by Andy, our guide. I found out that every boat that travels around the Galápagos Islands has a licensed guide who knows everything about these islands and the creatures who fly, crawl and swim here.

Andy says we'll spend most of our days on shore walking around the islands, looking at the creatures – mostly birds and reptiles. Sometimes we'll swim from a beach, and sometimes we'll jump off the boat into the water. A few people plan to scuba dive, including Grandma! She says she wants to dive with fish that are found only here. And she wants to look at hammerhead sharks, huge manta rays, and sea turtles.

Still Day One, Later

Dear Diary,

We are anchored close to land. Dozens of sea lions doze and sun on the shore. Others play in the water.

I jumped off the boat and got a big surprise! Even though it's broiling hot in the middle of the day, the waters of the Galápagos Islands feel real cold.

Grandma snorkeled with me.

I saw yellow-tailed surgeonfish beneath me – there must have been a hundred of them!

Suddenly a big body – then another – bolted past us. Grandma and I were quickly surrounded by *ten* adorable young sea lions!

It was a circus in the sea! Sea lion pups dived beneath us, blowing silvery bubbles through their noses. They somersaulted and flipped themselves into pretzel shapes. They chased and nipped each other. They are like big kittens. They seemed to be showing off just for us. They never scared me.

But the big male sea lion on shore did scare me with his bellowing roar! The other sea lions answered the bull with barks and coughing and burping sounds.

Andy told us that the bull sea lions try to keep other males away. They also keep watch for sharks.

Day Two
Santa Cruz

Dear Diary,

This morning we anchored in Academy Bay off Santa Cruz, one of the four islands in the Galápagos Islands where people live.

I'm so excited! After lunch I'm going to see giant Galápagos tortoises – the largest land tortoises in the world! At the Charles Darwin Research Station I'll get to see them up really close. Grandma says the station was named for Charles Darwin, who sailed to the Galápagos in 1835 on the ship the *Beagle* and later became a famous scientist. (I just found out that *galápagos* means tortoise in old Spanish.)

Later

Dear Diary,

I am so mad I could cry!

Long ago, explorers, pirates and seal and whale hunters came here. The fresh meat of the giant tortoise kept them from starving to death. The sailors knew that tortoises can stay alive for a year without food or water, so they stacked them by the hundreds in the damp, dark holds of their ships.

Rats are no friends of tortoise, either. There were never rats here until the ships brought them. The rats swam to shore and began to destroy tortoise eggs and young tortoises. No wonder there are so few giant tortoises left.

The good news is that today, thanks to the Charles Darwin Research Station and the National Park Service, a lot of giant tortoises are being saved.

Before bedtime

Dear Diary,

I saw them! I couldn't believe my eyes! I had read that giant tortoises can weigh over 500 pounds so I wasn't expecting a little box turtle. But I never dreamed there would be such big tortoises. And they looked so old with their great wrinkled necks and teary eyes.

I love Galápagos tortoises more than anything.

(Extract from *Swimming with Sea Lions* by Ann McGovern. Copyright © 1992 Ann McGovern, published by Scholastic Inc.)

VERBS

A verb is a *doing* word. It tells us what people, animals and things do. Verbs also tells us about the time at which things were done. For example, verbs that tell us what people, animals and things are doing *now*, are in the *present tense*. Here is a list of all the parts of the verb 'to walk':

	SINGULAR	PLURAL
1st person	I walk	We walk
2nd person	You walk	You walk
3rd person	He/she/it walks	They walk

Verbs that tell us what people, animals and things did in the *past* are in the *past tense*. Most verbs add '-ed' to show that they are in the past tense:

	SINGULAR	PLURAL
1st person	I walked	We walked
2nd person	You walked	You walked
3rd person	He/she/it walked	They walked

■ Write out the present and past tense of the following verbs, using the example above as a model:

open	call	shout
thank	look	heal

■ Do the same with these verbs. What is different about them?

say	sting	come
have	leave	fly

These verbs are called *irregular* verbs because each one is different.

READING COMPREHENSION

PART A

■ Answer the following questions:

1. How did Ann and her Grandma get to the Galápagos islands?
2. Who is Andy, and how did he help them?
3. List all the different kinds of creatures mentioned in the diary.
4. What surprised Ann when she jumped in the sea for the first time?
5. Which famous scientist visited the islands in 1835?
6. What does the name 'Galápagos' mean?
7. What threatens the survival of the giant tortoises?
8. What surprised Ann when she saw her first giant tortoise?

PART B

■ Underline the verbs in these sentences:

Today I walked right up to birds.

A few people plan to scuba dive.

Sea lions play in the water.

They chased and nipped each other.

I love Galápagos tortoises more than anything.

The rats swam to shore.

Are the verbs you underlined in the past or present tense?

■ Circle the present tense verbs in red. Circle the past tense verbs in blue.

■ Underline in green all the adjectives you can find in Ann's diary.

■ Underline Ann's personal thoughts, feelings and expressions of surprise in purple.

PART C

■ Use the library, CD-ROMs or the Internet to research one of the following:

• Charles Darwin
• The Galápagos Islands
• Sea lions.

DIARY WRITING

OBJECTIVES

UNIT	SPELLING/VOCABULARY	GRAMMAR/PUNCTUATION	COMPREHENSION/ COMPOSITION
WRITING NON-FICTION Recount (Diary): Extract from *Searching for Laura Ingalls* by Kathryn Lasky and Meribah Knight.	Spell and punctuate contractions.	Diary style: personal expression, 1st-person recount.	Write 1st-person recount: diary.

ORGANIZATION (1 HOUR)

	INTRODUCTION	WHOLE-CLASS SKILLS WORK	DIFFERENTIATED GROUP ACTIVITIES	CONCLUSION
HOUR 1	Introduce and read extract.	Exercise on contractions.	1–3: Write detailed diary entry for something that happened in the last day or two. 4*: As above, but with support from the teacher.	Share examples of the diaries.

RESOURCES

Photocopiable pages 51 ('Searching for Laura Ingalls') and 52 (Contractions), OHP and acetate (optional), writing materials.

PREPARATION

Prepare enough copies of pages 51 and 52 for one between two children. Prepare these as OHTs as well, if possible. Otherwise, enlarge them on the photocopier to at least A3 size.

Introduction

Share the background information to 'Searching for Laura Ingalls' written in italics on page 51. Read on, pointing out the qualities of the writing in the first two paragraphs.

> *I finally had my dream come true, but it was almost a bad dream, a nightmare. I got to go wading and swimming in Plum Creek.*
> *It was warm and the current in the creek was going really fast. When I waded into the water I fell, but I got used to it and started to swim. When I stood up my clothes were heavy and wet. I felt like stones were hanging on my skirt. I climbed trees that were sticking out over the creek.*

Explain that it is detailed, descriptive and expresses the writer's thoughts and feelings. It is also written in a friendly, personal and informal style. Ask the children to find examples of these qualities in the last paragraph.

> *But guess what? When I came out of Plum Creek I saw this thing that looked like a glob of mud on my foot, and then I thought, It's a black slug, but then I thought, Slugs aren't black. Then I remembered. It came back all awful. It was a leech just like the ones Laura got on her. I had forgotten this whole part of the book, the part about the leeches. My stomach flip-flopped, my brain went crazy, and I started to scream. Of course my dad just had to take a picture before he pulled it off me.*

Whole-class skills work

Explain that contractions are often used in speech, and are appropriate to some kinds of informal writing, such as diaries. Work through the exercises on the photocopiable page 52 (Contractions).

Differentiated group activities

1–3: Ask the children to write a detailed diary entry for something that happened to them in the last day or two. Explain that the more recent the event they choose, the better, because they will be able to remember it in greater detail. The event can be something quite ordinary – most diary entries are – but it is important that they should write it in the same way that Meribah Knight (and Ann McGovern in *Swimming with Sea Lions*) wrote hers. They need to express personal thoughts and feelings in a relaxed, chatty style.

4*: As above, but children should concentrate on writing a good, but *short*, diary entry with the support of the teacher.

Conclusion

Share some of the diary entries. Encourage children to listen carefully and say how far each one includes the qualities discussed in the Introduction. Finally, ask children to keep a diary for a week (or longer), then bring them into school to share with the class. Give particular praise to detailed, descriptive writing which reveals personal thoughts and feelings.

FOLLOW-UP (1 HOUR)

See page 203 which provides a grid plan for a 1-hour follow-up unit based on Chapter 4 ('Deep Water') of *On the Banks of Plum Creek* by Laura Ingalls Wilder.

SEARCHING FOR LAURA INGALLS

A girl called Meribah Knight loved the books written by Laura Ingalls Wilder so much that she wished she could visit some of the places in them. After reading On the Banks of Plum Creek *she dreamed of swimming in the same creek as Laura did. One summer her wish came true when she travelled there, in a campervan, with her family. This is how Meribah described Plum Creek in her diary.*

I finally had my dream come true, but it was almost a bad dream, a nightmare. I got to go wading and swimming in Plum Creek.

It was warm and the current in the creek was going really fast. When I waded into the water I fell, but I got used to it and started to swim. When I stood up my clothes were heavy and wet. I felt like stones were hanging on my skirt. I climbed trees that were sticking out over the creek.

I remembered in the book how Laura went to look under branches and rocks for the old crab, the one she used to scare Nellie Oleson, the stuck-up girl in the book. I looked for it, too. I couldn't find it, so I swam along some more and hung from branches.

But guess what? When I came out of Plum Creek I saw this thing that looked like a glob of mud on my foot, and then I thought, It's a black slug, but then I thought, Slugs aren't black. Then I remembered. It came back all awful. It was a leech just like the ones Laura got on her. I had forgotten this whole part of the book, the part about the leeches. My stomach flip-flopped, my brain went crazy, and I started to scream. Of course my dad just had to take a picture before he pulled it off me.

(Extract from *Searching for Laura Ingalls: A Reader's Journey* by Kathryn Lasky and Meribah Knight.)

CONTRACTIONS

Sometimes two words are joined together in a shorter form. We often use these shorter forms in conversation and informal writing.

LONG FORM	SHORTENED FORM
is not	isn't
cannot	can't
you are	you're
do not	don't

The apostrophe (') is put in to show where letters have been missed out.

REMEMBER: **Don't** make the common mistake of placing it where the gap between the words used to be: It should be **shouldn't** NOT **should'nt!**

■ Write the long form of these words:

I'm
she's
mustn't
they're
we've
you'll
should've
mightn't

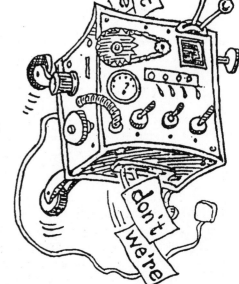

■ Write the shortened form of these words:

she had
they have
he will
we are
he is
Dad will
who has
would not

Here is an unusual one: will not.
Do you know what the shortened form is?

■ Find some examples of contractions in *Searching for Laura Ingalls* and other texts.

USING A THESAURUS

OBJECTIVES

UNIT	SPELLING/VOCABULARY	GRAMMAR/PUNCTUATION	COMPREHENSION/ COMPOSITION
REFERENCE AND RESEARCH SKILLS Using a thesaurus.	Understand the meaning of the words 'thesaurus' and 'synonym'.	Understand what a synonym is. Investigate how the changing of words in a sentence has an impact on meaning.	Understand the purpose and organization of a thesaurus. Make use of a thesaurus to find synonyms.

ORGANIZATION (1 HOUR)

INTRODUCTION	WHOLE-CLASS SKILLS WORK	DIFFERENTIATED GROUP ACTIVITIES	CONCLUSION
Read a short fable by Aesop and investigate how the writing can be improved by using synonyms.	Understand what a thesaurus is and how to use one.	1*: Work on a piece of own writing, finding synonyms to improve it. 2 & 3: Work on fable, finding synonyms for selected words to improve it. 4*: As above, with teacher support.	Select pupils from Groups 2 & 3 to read out their writing. Evaluate and discuss how they were able to improve on the original.

RESOURCES

Photocopiable page 55 ('The Fox and the Crow'), short pieces of writing in draft form already done by children in Group 1, thesauruses, OHP and acetate (optional).

PREPARATION

If possible, prepare an OHT (or A3 enlargement) of photocopiable page 55 ('The Fox and the Crow'). Make enough copies to have one between two for children in Groups 2–4, then adapt the sheet by underlining the words for which the children should find synonyms – more for Groups 2 and 3, than for Group 4.

Introduction

Display the story of 'The Fox and the Crow'. You might wish to explain to the children that it is a retold version of a fable by Aesop, and remind them that a fable is a short story that teaches a lesson about life.

Read the story and discuss briefly what the 'moral' might be. Then focus the children's attention on the way the story has been written. How could it be improved? Point out to them the repetition of the word 'said' and the lack of descriptive quality in the choice of words like 'nice', 'happy', 'get' and so on. Ask the children to suggest other words that could be used instead.

Introduce the word 'synonym' and establish that a synonym is a word that has almost the same meaning as another word. Often when we are writing we would want to use a synonym in order to:

- avoid repetition
- say more precisely what we mean
- create an image.

Whole-class skills work

Say a word, such as 'big', and ask the children to come up with synonyms (*large, huge, immense, enormous* and so on). When they've exhausted their supply, ask: Where could we find more synonyms for 'big'? Hold up a thesaurus and explain that it is a dictionary of synonyms. Demonstrate how to use it to find words to replace those you've highlighted in the fable.

Differentiated group activities

1*: In pairs, children should read a piece written by their partner and suggest at least five words that might be replaced with a synonym to make the writing more effective. The writer then uses a thesaurus to find alternatives. In addition they should be encouraged to find further, or better, adjectives and adverbs.

2 & 3: In pairs, children work on the Aesop tale to find effective synonyms for the words highlighted by the teacher.

4*: As above, but with teacher support.

Conclusion

Ask selected children from Groups 2 and 3 to read out their revised fables. As a class, evaluate and discuss how they improved on the original.

USING A THESAURUS

One nice day a crow was sitting up in a tree. As she looked around she saw some cheese lying on the ground.

'That looks good,' said the crow. So she flew down, picked up the cheese with her mouth and flew back into the tree.

Just then a fox walked by. He was very hungry. He saw the crow and wanted the cheese for himself.

'Let me have that cheese,' he said to the crow loudly. The crow shook her head.

'How can I get that cheese?' the fox said to himself. 'I cannot get up the tree, so I will have to think of a good plan.' And he did.

'You are a very pretty bird,' he said to the crow. 'What a nice black coat of feathers you have.' The crow was very happy.

'And I hear you have a very pretty voice, too. Please, let me hear you sing,' said the fox.

The crow was so happy that she didn't stop to think. She opened her mouth and began to sing. And what happened then, do you think? Of course, the cheese came out of her mouth, and the fox was there quickly to get it.

It's true what they say about foxes: they really are clever!

'The Fox and the Crow'
Retold from *Aesop's Fables*

THE MONTHS OF THE YEAR

OBJECTIVES

UNIT	SPELLING/VOCABULARY	GRAMMAR/PUNCTUATION	COMPREHENSION/ COMPOSITION
READING POETRY Classic poem: 'The Months of the Year' by Sara Coleridge.	Recognize one- and two-syllable rhymes. Spell the months of the year.	Use grammatical knowledge to reassemble text. Revise adjectives.	Identify couplets. Demonstrate comprehension by resequencing.

ORGANIZATION (2 HOURS)

	INTRODUCTION	WHOLE-CLASS SKILLS WORK	DIFFERENTIATED GROUP ACTIVITIES	CONCLUSION
HOUR 1	Read 'The Months of the Year' on photocopiable page 58.	Investigate rhyme. Introduce the term 'couplet'. Identify couplets in the poem.	1–3: Resequence a cut-up version of the poem. 4*: Resequence a simpler cut-up version of the poem.	Re-read the poem. Selected pupils recite part of the poem from memory.
HOUR 2	Re-read 'The Months of the Year'.	Spell the months of the year. Revise adjectives. Find adjectives in the poem.	1*: Write own second line to each verse. 2 & 3: Add adjectives in blank spaces. 4*: As above, but with support.	Selected pupils read out their own version of the poem.

RESOURCES

Photocopiable page 58 ('The Months of the Year'), board or flip chart, OHP and acetate (optional), scissors (one pair between two), paste, blank paper, writing materials.

PREPARATION

One copy of the complete poem on photocopiable page 58 is needed for the teacher's reference, plus a few spares for the children to use. Prepare also an OHT if possible. For the sequencing exercise, prepare cut-up versions as follows:
■ For Groups 1 to 3, cut up each line of the poem, shuffle, then paste down in random order. Photocopy enough for one between two. The children put the first lines in order using the names of the months, then match up the second lines using the rhymes.
■ For Group 4, blank out the second lines of each verse and photocopy enough for one between two. This sheet will also be needed for another purpose in Hour 2. On another sheet, provide all the second lines in jumbled-up form.
■ Finally, prepare a version of the poem with all the adjectives blanked out. Copy enough for one between two.

Introduction

Introduce the poet with some brief background information. (Sara Coleridge was a mid-nineteenth-century poet. She was married to Samuel Taylor Coleridge who was also a poet, but much more famous of the two!) Read the poem 'The Months of the Year'. Re-read it, pausing where necessary to explain the meanings of difficult words.

Whole-class skills work

Write the first couplet of the poem on the board or flip chart and ask the children to identify the rhyme. Ask the following questions: 'What is rhyme?' 'Which part of each word actually rhymes?' Then brainstorm and jot down more -*ow* rhymes. (If children suggest -*ow* words such as *now, cow, how,* explain that the letters -*ow* make a different sound in those words.) Do the same with verse 7, asking 'How many syllables in "showers" and "flowers"?' 'How many syllables rhyme?' Explain that these are two-syllable rhymes.

Differentiated group activities

All children work in pairs within groups.
1–3: Give out copies of the jumbled up lines (see 'Preparation') and ask children to cut them out, resequence them and paste down their final version. Tell them to find the months of the year first, then put them in order. Finally, ask the children to find the rhymes that go with these lines.
4*: Give out the prepared sheet which has the second line of each verse blanked out, plus the sheet of jumbled-up second lines. The children should cut up the lines on this second sheet and paste them underneath the correct first lines using the rhymes as a guide.

Conclusion

Read out the poem again and ask the children to check their versions against this. Invite them to attempt to recite part of the poem from memory. After working intensively with the poem in this way, some children will be able to this. Before the end of the session, tell the children to revise the months of the year spellings for homework.

Introduction

Read 'The Months of the Year' poem together. Then divide the class in two and ask the two groups to read alternate verses. Get the children to say each of the months out loud in order, picking up on the syllabic rhythms. Clap the syllables. Select children to come up and write the months on the board.

Whole-class skills work

Revise understanding of the term 'adjective' in a quick question and answer session. Ask the children to find the adjectives in their pasted-up version of the poem (if any pupil's version is too messy for this, give them one of the spares prepared earlier). The teacher will need to support Group 4 during this session.

At the end of the session, quickly go through the adjectives in the poem. They are: *verse 2*: frozen; *verse 3*: loud, shrill, dancing; *verse 4*: sweet; *verse 5*: pretty, fleecy; *verse 7*: cooling; *verse 9*: warm; *verse 10*: fresh; pleasant; *verse 11*: dull; *verse 12*: chill, blazing, Christmas.

Differentiated group activities

1*: Work on copies of the poem from which all the second lines of verses have been deleted (see 'Preparation'). They should attempt to write in their own second lines. Explain that, if they are really stuck ('lambs' is a bit of a problem rhyme!), they can use or adapt what Sara Coleridge wrote.
2 & 3: Work in pairs on a copy of the poem from which all the adjectives have been deleted. Write in adjectives of their own.
4*: As above, but supported by the teacher.

Conclusion

Selected children read out their own version of the poem. For Group 1, this will be a version with different second lines to each verse, and for the rest of the class, a version with different adjectives.

FURTHER IDEAS

■ Ask the children to try to learn the poem by heart.
■ Ask the children to look through poetry books to find other examples of poems with couplets. These could be collected together in a wall display or class anthology.
■ The 'text-processing' in the two hours above could be repeated with similar rhyming poems later in the year.

THE MONTHS OF THE YEAR

January brings the snow;
Makes our feet and finger glow.

February brings the rain,
Thaws the frozen ponds again.

March brings breezes, loud and shrill,
Stirs the dancing daffodil.

April brings the primrose sweet,
Scatters daisies at our feet.

May brings flocks of pretty lambs,
Skipping by their fleecy dams.

June brings tulips, lilies, roses;
Fills the children's hands with posies.

Hot July brings cooling showers,
Strawberries and gilly-flowers.

August brings the sheaves of corn,
Then the Harvest home is borne.

Warm September brings the fruit,
Sportsmen then begin to shoot.

Fresh October brings the pheasant;
Then to gather nuts is pleasant.

Dull November brings the blast,
Then the leaves are falling fast.

Chill December brings the sleet,
Blazing fire and Christmas treat.

Sara Coleridge

dams	mothers
posies	bunches of flowers
gilly-flowers	scented pink flowers
sheaves	stacks of corn
pheasant	a kind of game bird

ACROSTIC POEMS

OBJECTIVES

UNIT	SPELLING/VOCABULARY	GRAMMAR/PUNCTUATION	COMPREHENSION/COMPOSITION
WRITING POETRY Acrostic poems.	Understand alphabetical order.	Understand that the unit of poetry is the line and that poetry does not have to rhyme (free verse).	Write short, free-verse poems to the pattern provided by an acrostic.

ORGANIZATION (1 HOUR)

	INTRODUCTION	WHOLE-CLASS SKILLS WORK	DIFFERENTIATED GROUP ACTIVITIES	CONCLUSION
HOUR 1	Display and read the examples of acrostics on photocopiable page 61. Ask if pupils can spot anything interesting about them.	Explain how to write an acrostic poem. Demonstrate how a dictionary can be used to help to find words. Revise alphabetical order.	Start with simple practice acrostics: Group 1*: Attempt long words. Groups 2 & 3*: Attempt words of six to eight letters. Group 4*: Attempt words of three or four letters.	Read examples selected from the whole class.

RESOURCES

Photocopiable page 61 (Acrostic Poems), board or flip chart, OHP and acetate (optional), enough dictionaries for one between four (if available, simple dictionaries normally used for Key Stage 1 children are preferable, as they will contain shorter lists of more useful words).

PREPARATION

Either photocopy the top half of photocopiable page 61 ('Rainbow' and 'Vampire' poems) enough for one between two children, or prepare an OHT of these poems.

Introduction

Display the 'Rainbow' and 'Vampire' acrostic poems on an OHP, or hand out copies of them, and ask if the children can spot anything interesting about them. Give them clues if necessary until someone has spotted that the first letter of each line makes a word when read downwards. Explain that this is called an 'acrostic'.

Whole-class skills work

Demonstrate how to write an acrostic poem. Start by writing the word 'SUN' downwards on the board, then show how each line can be completed, using this example:

So bright
Up in the sky
Nice and hot.

Point out that the lines should not be too long (no longer than one line of the children's own paper).

Demonstrate how a dictionary can be used to help find words for writing acrostic poems. Spend a few minutes revising alphabetical order, perhaps using a quiz form.

Differentiated group activities

Groups 1–4*: All start with simple practice acrostics, ranging from words of three to four letters for Group 4, to words of nine to ten letters for Group 1. After the practice session, the children should try longer and/or more expressive acrostics. All children will need help from time to time during this activity, but Group 4 is likely to need additional support.

Conclusion

Select children from each group to share their work with the rest of the class. Since the poems will be read aloud rather than displayed, ask the class to listen carefully to the first letter of each line. Can they guess the acrostic? For acrostics using longer words, ask the class poets to read their poems a second time and ask another child to come up and write the first letter of each line on the board. Can the children guess the word before it is completed?

FOLLOW-UP (1 HOUR)

See page 204 which provides a grid plan for a 1-hour follow-up unit on writing acrostic variations.

ACROSTIC POEMS

Rainbow

Rain and sun together make the rainbow grow
Arching in the cloudy sky, see the colours glow.
Indigo and violet, bands of red and blue,
Now it's bold and brilliant, then it fades from view.
Bridge of coloured ribbons – magic to behold
Over field and factory...over wood and wold.
Where the rainbow comes to earth
       – there's the crock of gold.

David Whitehead

Vampire

Vicious beings in the night,
A bat swoops past your head,
Maybe it's not what it seems,
Perhaps it's your Uncle George instead.
I always thought him rather funny,
Reading books whilst standing upside-down –
Easy for a vampire!

Claire Gunn

School daze

Our	School days start with playground noise,
with	Children racing, shouting boys.
Now	Here's the teacher bang on time;
he	Opens jaws, 'Get into line!'
But	Outside the gate a last girl crawls.
'Ann!	Late again!' the teacher bawls.
Then	Doors slam shut, and classrooms shake.
Our	All-action school is wide awake.
Some	Zoos, I think, have calmer ways
but we	Effect a real school daze.

Wes Magee

Brilliant mini-sun
     under man's control
lacking the candle's loveliness –
     but a lot brighter!

Chris Webster

REMOTE CONTROL KID

OBJECTIVES

UNIT	SPELLING/VOCABULARY	GRAMMAR/PUNCTUATION	COMPREHENSION/ COMPOSITION
READING PLAYS 'Remote Control Kid'.	Understand and use vocabulary related to drama conventions.	Mark up a text to support reading aloud. Identify statements, questions, orders and exclamations.	Read a playscript with expression. Respond imaginatively to character and plot. Make simple notes.

ORGANIZATION (3 HOURS)

	INTRODUCTION	WHOLE-CLASS SKILLS WORK	DIFFERENTIATED GROUP ACTIVITIES	CONCLUSION
HOUR 1	Look over the playscript on pages 65 and 66 with pupils, explaining how to use it.	Explain the importance of expression in reading. Practise exercise in pairs.	1–4*: Read the play in mixed-ability groups of four or five.	Selected group reads Scene 1 and another group reads Scene 2. The rest of the class evaluates the readings.
HOUR 2	Explain the term 'blocking'.	Identify statements, questions, order and exclamations.	1–4*: In mixed-ability groups, pupils discuss ideas and plan their blocking on paper. They then try out their blocking, and rehearse the play.	Two different groups present their blocked version of the play. The rest of the class evaluates.
HOUR 3	Discuss further possible scenes/ episodes. Explain improvisation as a means of furthering script.	Model the 'blocking' process and the different ways of making blocking notes on playscript.	1–4*: Allocate each mixed-ability group a scenario to improvise.	Groups who have not yet performed to the class present their improvisations. The rest of the class evaluates.

RESOURCES

Photocopiable pages 65 and 66 ('Remote Control Kid'), a large space (drama studio or hall, if available, otherwise, a classroom with tables pushed out of the way), some chairs, two boxes to represent a television and video, a calculator (optional), OHP and acetate (optional).

PREPARATION

Make enough copies of the play on photocopiable pages 65 and 66 for one per child and, if possible, prepare OHTs of the script. Alternatively, enlarge each sheet to A3 size. Prepare a performance area at the front of the studio, hall or classroom. This should contain some chairs and two boxes to represent a television and video. A calculator will make an excellent 'remote control'.

Introduction

Examine the photocopiable playscript with the children, using OHTs or an enlarged version. Discuss which features of a playscript format distinguish it from a story. Explain that scene descriptions are usually in italics and stage directions are always in italics and brackets, and should not normally be read out.

Whole-class skills work

Explain the importance of expression in reading, particularly in plays. Give the children an exercise to do in pairs: ask them to say the line, 'It's raining!' in three different ways. These include: you are disappointed that it is raining because it will spoil your day out; you are pleased it is raining because your flower bed is parched; you are surprised that it is raining because it has been hot and dry for two weeks. Try other phrases in the same way. Discuss ways of marking expression on the text.

Now move on to explain that there are four types of sentence: statements, questions, orders and exclamations:

- Statements end with a full stop and a falling intonation (tone of voice).
- Questions end with a question mark and a rising intonation.
- Orders end with a full stop or exclamation mark and have a level, 'clipped' intonation.
- Exclamations end with an exclamation mark and have a high, rising intonation.

Ask the children to identify some examples of each of these in the text and practise reading them with the correct intonation.

Differentiated group activities

1–4*: Provide each child with a copy of the playscript. Note that all groupings for this unit are mixed-ability groups of four. If a group of five is necessary because of total numbers, the fifth person should be a narrator and read all the text appearing in italics. Children from Group 4 should be allocated the part of Tom as this has the fewest and simplest lines (though it is also the star role!).

The first task of each group is to allocate the other parts. Tell the children not to try to match gender (for example, Mum can be a boy or a girl). Groups should then read the play several times, concentrating on developing realistic expression. Encourage the children to mark their text with reminders to aid their expression. They could also underline or highlight their part just as real actors do. During the session, the teacher gives organizational support to all groups.

Conclusion

One group should be chosen to read Scene 1 and another to read Scene 2. The rest of the class should evaluate the readings by commenting on how true to life the readers' expression was, and giving suggestions for improvement.

Introduction

Explain to the class that they are going to plan out the movements of the characters for the play and that this is called 'blocking'. When movements are being planned, the position of the audience must be kept in mind to ensure that they have a clear view of everything that happens and that the actors are facing the audience as much as possible.

Arrange the front of the studio, hall or classroom as a simple performance area (see 'Preparation'). Though only one group will be able to rehearse in it at a time, all groups should plan with that space in mind.

Whole-class skills work

Model the process of determining blocking by asking the children to brainstorm ideas for actors' movements in the first part of Scene 1. Remind them that they must think carefully about what the characters are saying and to whom, so that their movements are realistic. Then ask how the blocking ideas might be indicated on the script. Suggest the use of notes and/or symbols, for example: move →; **X** to Dad.

Differentiated group activities

1–4*: Each mixed-ability group should plan its ideas and make notes on paper before beginning to try them out in the space allocated. All groups should try out their blocking, and then rehearse the whole script a number of times. The teacher gives support where required.

Conclusion

Ask two different groups to present their version of the fully-blocked play in the performance area. The other children should be encouraged to evaluate the blocking: Can they see what is happening? Do the movements help to put across the meaning of the words? Can all the actors be heard clearly?

HOUR 3

Introduction

Suggest that the script is only the first part of a play. Tell the children that they will have to improvise their own ending. Explain the term 'improvisation', saying that it means 'making it up as you go along'. Tell the children that it is a technique often used by actors for practice, and also in performance as a way of creating true-to-life dialogue.

Whole-class skills work

Model the improvisation technique for the whole class by inviting two children to the front of the class. Give them a scenario to improvise, for example: 'You are late getting to school and your teacher wants to know why.' Prompt them when necessary and make it clear that improvisation requires careful listening since partners have to respond realistically to what each says. In pairs, get the class to work on the following improvisation: 'A friend wants to borrow a pound, but you do not really want to lend it.'

Differentiated group activities

1–4*: Allocate one of the following improvisations to each mixed-ability group and give support as necessary:
■ What will Trish do when she gets her turn on the remote control?
■ What happens at school next day?
■ What happens on school sports day?
■ What happens when Tom walks past someone playing with a remote control aeroplane or boat?
■ How does Tom get back to normal?

Conclusion

Groups who have not performed before, present their improvisations to the class followed by evaluation. Finally, explain that any one or two of the improvisations followed by getting Tom back to normal would complete the play.

FURTHER IDEAS

Each group could work out its own complete version of the play and prepare to present it without scripts. The children could also go on to turn the play into a story. This would provide a valuable exercise in punctuating and setting out dialogue. The next unit, 'Little Red Riding Hood 2000' on page 67, deals with writing playscripts and provides an ideal follow-up.

REMOTE CONTROL KID

CAST: Mum, Dad, Tom, Trish

SCENE 1: *The lounge in the Rackitt's house. Tom is gobbling a packet of sweets. Dad is trying to fix the remote control for the video. Trish is watching TV. Mum is in the kitchen, off stage.*

Mum:	(*From off stage*) Tom, come and help me with the dinner!
Tom:	In a sec, I'm just finishing my sweets.
Mum:	Sweets? You shouldn't be eating sweets before your dinner!
Dad:	Tom, come and help me to mend this remote control.
Tom:	OK, Dad.
Dad:	Here, hold this. It's the microchip that makes it work.
Tom:	OK, Dad.
Dad:	Mind you be careful with it.
Tom:	OK, Dad.

(Tom holds the microchip in one hand and a handful of sweets in the other. He puts the wrong hand to his mouth by mistake and swallows the chip.)

Tom:	(*In a loud wail*) Ooops!
Dad:	What's up?
Tom:	(*Choking*) I just swallowed the chip.
Mum:	(*Rushing into the room*) Quick, call the doctor!
Trish:	(*Moaning*) Oh no, now I can't watch my new video!
Dad:	Stop fussing. It won't hurt him. It was no bigger than one of his sweets.
Mum:	Right. Come and get your dinner, then.
Tom:	What is it?
Mum:	Toad in the hole and Brussels sprouts.
Trish } Tim }:	(*Together*) Yuk!

SCENE 2: *The next day. Mum, Trish and Tom are in the lounge. Dad enters with a new remote control.*

Dad:	I've got the new remote!
Trish:	Great! Can I use it?
Dad:	I just want to test it first.
Trish:	Test it on my new video (*putting new video cassette in recorder*).
Dad:	OK, here goes. I'm pressing 'PLAY'...now! (*presses a button*)

(Tom starts to play with one of his toys.)

Trish:	(*Looking at TV*) It works!
Dad:	And I'm pressing 'STOP'...now! (*presses a button*)

(Tom stops playing with his toy.)

Trish: (*Looking at TV*) That works as well.
Dad: I'm pressing 'FAST FORWARD'...now! (*presses a button*)

(*Tom stands up and starts running around the room.*)

Trish: (*Looking at Tom*) Dad!
Dad: And I'm pressing 'REWIND'...now! (*presses a button*)

(*Tom starts running backwards around the room.*)

Trish: (*Looking at Tom*) Dad!
Dad: And now I'm pressing...'SEARCH'! (*presses a button*)

(*Tom stops running and starts looking for something.*)

Trish: (*Looking at Tom*) Dad, LOOK!!!
Dad: What is it?
Trish   It's Tom, that's what!
Dad: (*Looking at Tom*) He looks all right to me.
Trish   Well, he's not. When you press 'PLAY', he plays. And when you press 'STOP',
            he stops. And when you press...
Dad: Oh no! It must be that micro chip he swallowed. We must get it out. Quick, let's rush
            him to hospital!
Mum: Wait!

(*They both look at Mum.*)

Mum: He just might be a better behaved boy like this. Here, let me try.

(*She takes the remote control and presses a button.*)

Mum: Time for bed, Tom!

(*Tom runs outs of the room. We hear the sound of feet on the stairs, the brushing of teeth, etc.*)

Tom: (*Shouting from off stage*) I've cleaned my teeth, put my pyjamas on and got into bed.
            Night night, Mum.
Mum: (*Amazed*) What about that, eh? It usually takes hours of arguing!
Trish: This is great. I can press 'STOP' when he bullies me!
Dad: And we could let his teacher use it to make him work harder!
Mum: Terrific! We've got a remote control kid! He'll be no trouble now!

LITTLE RED RIDING HOOD 2000

OBJECTIVES

UNIT	SPELLING/VOCABULARY	GRAMMAR/PUNCTUATION	COMPREHENSION/COMPOSITION
WRITING PLAYS 'Little Red Riding Hood 2000'.	Spell common words which include the letter combinations *ph* and *ck*.	Recognize the difference between standard and non-standard English.	Write a play script using layout conventions correctly. Write convincing dialogue.

ORGANIZATION (2 HOURS)

	INTRODUCTION	WHOLE-CLASS SKILLS WORK	DIFFERENTIATED GROUP ACTIVITIES	CONCLUSION
HOUR 1	Display on an OHP the sample playscript on photocopiable page 69. Discuss what makes convincing dialogue.	Remind pupils of the conventions of setting out a playscript.	1*: Write a short play using the sample script as a model for setting it out. 2 & 3: Write an ending to the sample play. 4*: Write a short scene to add to the sample play.	Selected pupils read out their work.
HOUR 2	As above.	Learn some common words with silent letters.	1–4: All groups redraft their playscript. *The teacher supports Groups 2 & 3 in guided writing.	Other selected pupils read out their work.

RESOURCES

Photocopiable page 69 (Sample Playscript 'Little Red Riding Hood 2000'), board or flip chart, OHP and acetate (optional), writing materials.

PREPARATION

Make enough copies of photocopiable page 69 for one between two children. If possible, make an OHT of the photocopiable sheet.

Introduction

Display the sample playscript on photocopiable page 69 on an OHP or hand out a copy to each child. Explain to the children that the play is based on the story of Little Red Riding Hood, but is set in modern times. Tell them that it is the beginning of a play written by a child in her notebook.

Draw the children's attention to the layout of the playscript where the margin has been used for the characters' names. Read it through with appropriate expression, picking up on the modern language.

Discuss with the children how the dialogue reflects modern life, emphasizing particularly the importance of listening to the way people really speak in order to create realistic dialogue.

Whole-class skills work

Point out the key features of the script's layout: title, cast list (in order of appearance), 'scene' in capital letters, followed by a set description. The children should note that the set description is in the present tense, is brief, and is intended mainly to help the director plan out his set design and blocking. Character names should be written in the margin. Explain that dialogue begins immediately to the right of the margin and emphasize that it is not placed inside speech marks. Brief instructions to the actors are placed in brackets. Longer stage directions are preceded by a line space.

Differentiated group activities

Begin by working with Group 4, supporting them as they add a short, simple scene to the sample play. Point out that the length of the scene is not important. Explain that later (Hour 2), the children will have the chance to redraft their scene, paying close attention to the playscript conventions outlined above.

1*: Write a short play using the sample playscript as a model for setting out their work.
2 & 3: Write an ending to the sample play.
4*: Write a short scene to add to the sample play.

Conclusion

Selected children read out their work followed by discussion and evaluation.

Introduction

Display the sample playscript again on an OHP, or ask the children to look at their own copies to remind them of the conventions of setting out a playscript. Encourage them to refer to the sample play constantly as they redraft their own playscripts in group work time.

Whole-class skills work

Refer to the OHT and ask the children to find the words with the letters *ph* and *ck*. List them in two columns on the board or flip chart. Read the list of *ph* words (*photograph, phoned*) and establish that *ph* sounds like *f*. What do they notice about the word 'photograph'? (It begins and ends with *ph*!) Read the list of *ck* words (*rucksack, sick, clock, quickly, jacket, rock, wicked*). What do they notice about the letter *c* in these words? (It is silent.) Brainstorm other *ph* and *ck* words to add to the list. Choose a selection of these words for *Look, Say, Cover, Write and Check* practice.

Differentiated group activities

1–4: All groups redraft their playscript, referring closely to the sample playscript to remind them of the conventions used. The focus of this redrafting activity should be firmly on the clear and correct setting out of their script.
*The teacher supports Groups 2 and 3 in guided writing.

Conclusion

A selection of children who have not already read out are asked to read their scripts, followed by brief discussion and evaluation. Sum up the main conventions of setting out a playscript.

FURTHER IDEAS

The work in this unit is primarily an exercise in setting out playscripts. It should be reinforced as soon as possible by writing a script in which good quality plot and dialogue is the main focus, for example the improvised endings to the 'Remote Control Kid' unit could be written out.

SAMPLE PLAY SCRIPT

Little Red Riding Hood 2000

Cast: Mum, Little Red Riding Hood (LRRH)–(LBDJ), Wolf, Gran

SCENE 1: *Inside a cottage in the forest.*

Mum: *(Shouting)* Little Red Riding Hood!

LRRH: *(From upstairs)* Yes?

Mum: Will you take this rucksack of food and your school photograph to your sick Gran?

LRRH: Aw, Mum, I was just surfing the net!

Mum: You spend far too much time on that computer! Hurry up! I phoned Gran to say you'd be there by three o'clock.

(LRRH comes downstairs looking cross.)

Mum: Come on, quickly. Put your cloak and hood on.

LRRH: Aw, Mum, do I have to wear that old thing? It makes me look like something from a fairy story!

Mum: You know your Gran likes to see you in it.

LRRH: But Mum, it went out of fashion, like 300 years ago!

Mum: Your Gran used to wear one when she was your age.

LRRH: Yeah, like I said, 300 years ago! Can't I wear my blue denim jacket instead?

LBDJ: And can I be called 'Little Blue Denim Jacket' from now on?

Mum: Your Gran won't like it!

LBDJ: Tough! *(She sets off.)*

SCENE 2: *In the forest. It is dark and gloomy and wolves can be heard in the distance, but LBDJ is not worried because she can't hear them. She is wearing a portable CD player and her head is jigging up and down to the beat of the rock music. Suddenly, she sees the wicked wolf.*

Wolf: *(Trying to sound nice)* Good morning, Little Red Riding ...er, Little Blue...um...Denim...thing.

NOW HERE'S THE WEATHER...

OBJECTIVES

UNIT	SPELLING/VOCABULARY	GRAMMAR/PUNCTUATION	COMPREHENSION/COMPOSITION
READING NON-FICTION Report genre: Weather Forecast.	Develop and understand vocabulary relating to weather.	Introduce the simple future tense.	Read and understand a weather map and report. Compare the way that the information is presented. Put the forecast into writing following simple model.

ORGANIZATION (1 HOUR)

INTRODUCTION	WHOLE-CLASS SKILLS WORK	DIFFERENTIATED GROUP ACTIVITIES	CONCLUSION
Display the weather chart on photocopiable page 72 and help pupils to interpret using the key.	Explain the future tense using the auxiliary verb 'will'. Write out common verbs in the future tense.	1–4*: All pupils work in pairs within groups to complete the text for the weather map at their own level.	Selected pupils are asked to read out different sections of their forecasts. Look in newspapers, listen to TV/radio for weather forecasts as homework.

RESOURCES

Photocopiable page 72 (Weather Forecast), board or flip chart, OHP and acetate (optional), writing materials.

PREPARATION

If possible, prepare an OHT of photocopiable page 72, or enlarge it to A3 size. Then make enough copies for one sheet per child.

Introduction

Display the top part of the photocopiable weather chart (map and symbols) on an OHT or as an A3 enlargement. Discuss why we have weather forecasts and what sort of people in particular depend on weather forecasts. Where can we find weather forecasts? Encourage the children to think of all media sources that provide weather information (newspaper, radio, television, telephone, Internet and so on). Explain that the photocopiable sheet shows part of a weather forecast obtained from the Met Office by fax! Help the children to interpret the map using the key. Make sure they understand what all the symbols mean.

Reveal the bottom part of the page which has the beginning of a text report interpreting the map. Read this through and make sure the children see how the text reflects what is on the map.

Whole-class skills work

This is an ideal opportunity to introduce to the children the future tense, using the auxiliary verb 'will'. Write up on the board or flip chart the future tense of the verbs 'to have' and 'to be' used in the forecasts:

TO HAVE (future tense)

	SINGULAR	PLURAL
1st person:	I will have	We will have
2nd person:	You will have	You will have
3rd person:	He/she/it will have	They will have

TO BE (future tense)

	SINGULAR	PLURAL
1st person:	I will be	We will be
2nd person:	You will be	You will be
3rd person:	He/she/it will be	They will be

Then apply the pattern to other common verbs, for example *walk*, *go*, *try* and so on.

Differentiated group activities

Give out copies of the weather chart. All the children should work in pairs within their ability groups to complete the text for the weather map. The teacher provides support as appropriate. The first paragraph has been done as an example. Remind the children that they should mention the temperature, wind speed and direction. Also, if there are different things going on in a particular area, they should write about them, for example 'Scotland will have snow *and* rain in different areas'.

1*: Encourage children in this group to include as many details as possible. They should write on a separate sheet of paper to allow room for this.

2 & 3*: Complete the template as printed.

4*: If any children in this group are having difficulty, they should concentrate on the last paragraph – the weather for their own area.

Conclusion

Ask selected children to read out different sections of their forecasts. The rest of the class should evaluate how effectively they have turned the map into writing. Ask the children to look in a newspaper, or listen to the radio or watch the television to find a weather report as part of their homework.

WEATHER FORECAST

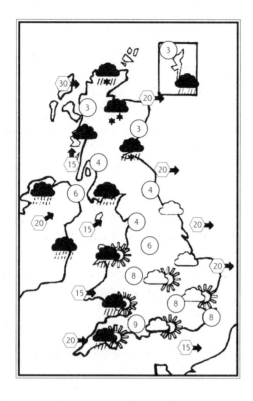

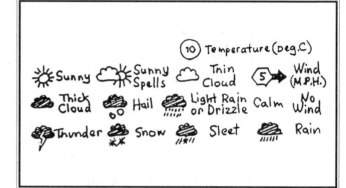

In England, the Midlands and South-East will have sunny spells.
The temperature will be around 8 degrees Celsius. The wind will come
from the east and will be fairly strong at around 20 miles per hour.

Wales and the West of England will have

Ireland will have

Scotland will have

The weather for our area will be

WEATHER REPORT

OBJECTIVES

UNIT	SPELLING/VOCABULARY	GRAMMAR/PUNCTUATION	COMPREHENSION/ COMPOSITION
WRITING NON-FICTION Report genre: Weather Report.	Use vocabulary appropriate to weather description.	Revise the simple future tense.	Plan and present a weather report.

ORGANIZATION (1 HOUR)

	INTRODUCTION	WHOLE-CLASS SKILLS WORK	DIFFERENTIATED GROUP ACTIVITIES	CONCLUSION
HOUR 1	Display the weather chart used in previous unit on page 75 as a model.	Revise the future tense using the auxiliary verb 'will' in the context of appropriate sentence patterns for a weather report.	1–4*: All pupils work in groups of four to plan a presentation of their weather forecast.	Selected groups present their forecast.

RESOURCES

Photocopiable page 75 (Weather Map), photocopiable page 72 (Weather Forecast) from previous unit, board or flip chart, OHP and acetate (if available), writing materials.

PREPARATION

The ideal preparation for this lesson is for the children to have done some weather research so that they can use relevant data, for example collecting data from a school weather station as part of science or geography work. If this is not possible, provide a fact sheet based on the current weather forecast in your area.

The evening before the lesson, ask the children to read, listen to and/or watch a weather report. Ask them to note the different types of information given and any interesting words used in describing the weather.

For the lesson, each group will need a copy of the Weather Map sheet on photocopiable page 75. You will also need an OHT or A3 enlargement of photocopiable page 72 (from the previous unit). If an OHP is available, some groups may wish to do their presentations on this. In this case, they will need an acetate of the Weather Map sheet.

Introduction

Discuss briefly the weather reports the children read, watched or listened to on the previous evening. Make a list of the information given (*temperature, wind speed and direction, wind chill factor, air quality, air pressure* and so on). Discuss these and any interesting words the children discovered (for example *blustery, gale force, drizzle, heat wave* and so on).

Then display the weather chart used in the previous unit as a model, either on the OHP or enlarged to A3 size. Explain that the children are going to write and present some weather forecasts. Be brief to allow them as much time as possible for their presentations.

Whole-class skills work

Revise the future tense of the verb 'to be' in the context of appropriate sentence patterns for a weather report. The best way to do this would be to look at work from the previous unit and ask the children to underline all the verbs in the future tense.

Differentiated group activities

The children should work in fours or fives within their larger-ability groups. The teacher provides support as appropriate.
1*: Produce newspaper presentations of their weather forecast as this is more demanding than the other two forms of presentation.
2 & 3*: Produce television presentations, using the OHP if possible.
4*: Produce radio presentations. These are the simplest of all because they are entirely verbal.

Conclusion

Selected groups present one of each type of forecast. The rest of the class evaluates how effectively the weather information was put across.

FURTHER IDEAS

Look at and listen to some more examples of real weather forecasts with the emphasis on what the presenters do to make the forecasts more interesting.
of fiction and non-fiction. Show also how the fiction and non-fiction shelves themselves are organized on the plan map. What other things besides books does the library have to

WEATHER MAP

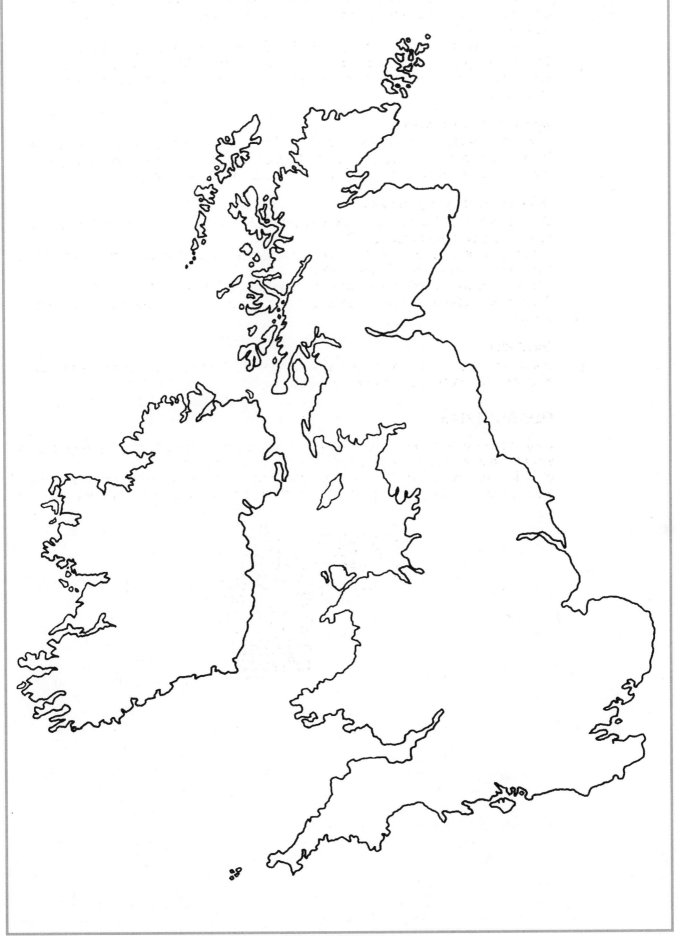

FACT OR FICTION?

OBJECTIVES

UNIT	SPELLING/VOCABULARY	GRAMMAR/PUNCTUATION	COMPREHENSION/COMPOSITION
REFERENCE AND RESEARCH SKILLS Fact or Fiction?	Develop vocabulary related to library use and organization.		Distinguish between fact and fiction and understand the difference. Know how and where to find fiction and non-fiction books in the school library.

ORGANIZATION (1 HOUR)

INTRODUCTION	WHOLE-CLASS SKILLS WORK	DIFFERENTIATED GROUP ACTIVITIES	CONCLUSION
Identify what pupils already know. Classify a collection of books as fiction or non-fiction. Establish definitions.	Use definitions to classify statements, extracts and book titles as fiction or non-fiction.	1–4: All groups visit the school library to find how it is organized. *The teacher supports Groups 2 & 3.	Share information. Make a master plan of the school library.

RESOURCES

A collection of fiction and non-fiction books, a collection of statements, extracts and illustrations from fiction and non-fiction books, access to the school library, board or flip chart, OHP and acetate (optional), writing materials.

PREPARATION

Collect a range of fiction and non-fiction books and prepare a collection of statements, extracts and illustrations from other fiction and non-fiction books to read and show during the whole-class skills session. Putting your collection on OHTs would be useful. Ensure that the school library is free for the differentiated group activities.

Introduction

Begin the session by holding up a fiction book and a non-fiction book and asking the children which is which. Write on the board or flip chart under the headings 'Fiction' and Non-fiction' what they already know about the differences between the two. Hold up more books and ask whether they would classify them as fiction on non-fiction. Explain that you now want to establish definitions for both 'fiction' and 'non-fiction'. Write up suggestions on the board or flip chart – and redraft until you are satisfied with your definitions. For example:

'Fiction books are made-up stories about people, places or things. They are usually written in the past tense and illustrated with pictures. You read them from beginning to end.'

'Non-fiction books tell facts about real things. They are usually written in the present tense and illustrated with photographs, maps, charts and diagrams. You usually read selected sections of them to find the information you want.'

Whole-class skills work

Test the definitions by holding up other books and reading out and showing children the statements, extracts and illustrations you have prepared – can they determine if these are fiction or non-fiction? This should be a fairly fast-paced activity.

Explain to all the children that in the next session, they will be visiting the school library to find out how it is organized and how they can find the books they want.

Differentiated group activities

Each child should have some paper and a pen or pencil. If the library will not comfortably accommodate the whole class at one time, work out a rota. The groups that are not in the library can examine how the books in the classroom are organized.

1: Draw a plan map of the library, noting how books are organized into separate sections of fiction and non-fiction. Show also how the fiction and non-fiction shelves themselves are organized on the plan map. What other things besides books does the library have to look at or read?

2 & 3*: As above, with teacher support.

4: Draw a plan map of the library showing where the fiction and non-fiction books are.

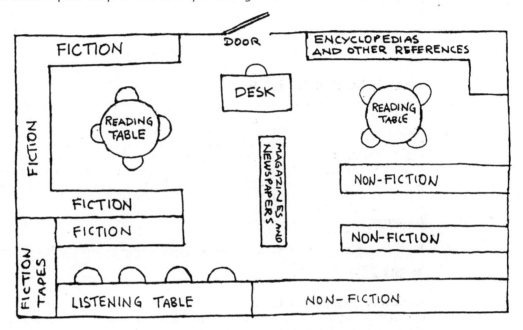

Conclusion

Ask selected children to share their maps with the rest of the class and compile a master version that can later be photocopied and given to each child as a handy resource. Discuss what they found out about how the library is organized. For example, fiction books are in one section of the library, and non-fiction books in another. Fiction books are put on the shelves in alphabetical order using the authors' last names. Non-fiction books are organized by subject matter. What else does the school library have besides books – what about newspapers, magazines, posters, CDs, audio cassette tapes and photographs?

SHAPE POEMS

OBJECTIVES

UNIT	SPELLING/VOCABULARY	GRAMMAR/PUNCTUATION	COMPREHENSION/COMPOSITION
WORD PLAY Shape poems.	Explore vocabulary related to poem's topic.	Investigate the impact of layout on meaning.	Explore shape poems.

ORGANIZATION (1 HOUR)

	INTRODUCTION	WHOLE-CLASS SKILLS WORK	DIFFERENTIATED GROUP ACTIVITIES	CONCLUSION
HOUR 1	Read the examples of shape poems on photocopiable page 80.	Write a shape poem as a class.	1–4: All pupils write own shape poem in their ability groups. *The teacher supports Group 4 in guided reading.	Share and evaluate poems.

RESOURCES

Photocopiable page 80 (Shape Poems), board or flip chart, OHP and acetate (optional), writing materials.

PREPARATION

If possible, prepare an OHT of photocopiable page 80 or enlarge the sheet to at least A3 size. Ideally, the three poems should be copied onto a page each so that they can be displayed separately, but this is not essential.

Introduction

Read the Michael Rosen poem about the rocket to the class without letting them see the layout. Then read it again slowly, emphasizing the descending and ascending numbers. Can the children imagine how the poem looks on the page? Write suggestions that the children make on the board or flip chart. Then display the poem (but do not show the other poems if these are on the same sheet). Is it anything like they imagined? Do the children think that seeing the poem before reading it would have made it easier to understand?

Establish that the poem is a shape poem. Explain to the children that in a shape poem, the words are arranged in a shape related to the subject of the poem. The layout helps the reader to see what the poem is about as well as to hear what it is about. Shape poems are often called 'concrete' poems. Finish by repeating the activity with the other two poems.

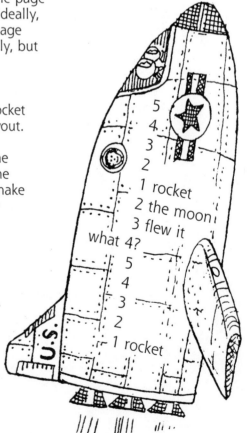

Whole-class skills work

Write a shape poem together as a class to model the process. First, brainstorm ideas for a shape and then choose the most popular one. Draw the shape on the board or flip chart. Then brainstorm again some words and phrases relevant to the chosen shape. Encourage the children to think of words and phrases that relate to all the scenes – sight, sound, touch, smell and taste (obviously dependent on the shape chosen).

When you feel you have a sufficient bank of words and phrases to draw on, work on fitting them into the shape in a way that flows well. Remind the children that they may well want to rewrite as they go along and this is fine. Just cross out, delete, insert and so on until everyone is happy with the result.

Differentiated group activities

All children should be working on creating their own shape poems.
1: Using suggestions from the brainstorming session or ideas of their own, the children work individually to create a shape poem.
2 & 3: As above, but working in pairs.
4*: Guided writing with the teacher to create a group poem.

Conclusion

Ask Group 4 to present their poem, both reading and displaying it. Select children from each of the other groups to do the same. Did anyone choose the same shape? If so, compare the two poems.

FURTHER IDEA

Outside of the literacy hour, ask the children to make a neat copy of their poems. Bind them into a class book, with a title such as 'Class 3 Shapes Up'. Children might like to take it in turns to take it home and share it with their families.

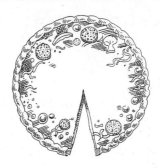

SHAPE POEMS

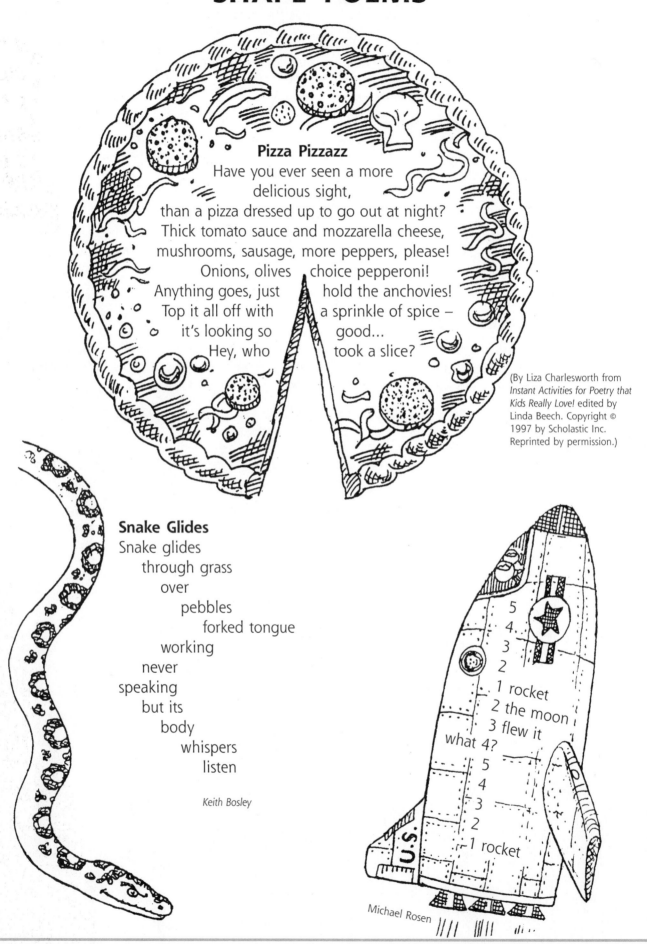

Pizza Pizzazz
Have you ever seen a more
delicious sight,
than a pizza dressed up to go out at night?
Thick tomato sauce and mozzarella cheese,
mushrooms, sausage, more peppers, please!
Onions, olives   choice pepperoni!
Anything goes, just   hold the anchovies!
Top it all off with   a sprinkle of spice –
it's looking so   good...
Hey, who   took a slice?

(By Liza Charlesworth from
*Instant Activities for Poetry that
Kids Really Love!* edited by
Linda Beech. Copyright ©
1997 by Scholastic Inc.
Reprinted by permission.)

Snake Glides
Snake glides
　　through grass
　　　　over
　　　　　　pebbles
　　　　　　　　forked tongue
　　　　working
　　never
speaking
　　but its
　　　　body
　　　　　　whispers
　　　　　　listen

Keith Bosley

5
4.
3
2
1 rocket
2 the moon
3 flew it
what 4?
5
4
3
2
1 rocket

U.S.

Michael Rosen

Term 2

PANDORA'S BOX

OBJECTIVES

UNIT	SPELLING/VOCABULARY	GRAMMAR/PUNCTUATION	COMPREHENSION/COMPOSITION
READING FICTION Myths and legends: 'Pandora's Box'.	Spell -f/ves plurals. Pronunciation of Greek names by syllables. Vocabulary in text.	Revision and reinforcement of previously taught skills, including capital letters, nouns, verbs etc. Understand differences between verbs in the 1st and 3rd person and relate to different text types.	Develop basic reading skills. Develop skills of prediction, inference and deduction. Write portrait of story character in form of letter.

ORGANIZATION (3 HOURS)

INTRODUCTION	WHOLE-CLASS SKILLS WORK	DIFFERENTIATED GROUP ACTIVITIES	CONCLUSION
HOUR 1 Read the story of 'Pandora's Box' on photocopiable page 85 aloud with the class, pausing at the end of part one (the asterisks) to discuss what might happen next.	Use the story as a basis for revision of skills covered to date: capital letters, nouns, adjectives, verbs, types of sentence, paragraphs, punctuation of speech, possessive apostrophe etc.	1*: Reading Comprehension, parts A & B. 2 & 3: Reading Comprehension, parts B & C. 4*: Reading Comprehension, part A.	Pupils from Group 1 present their reading of the first part of the story. Pupils from Group 4 present their reading of the second part.
HOUR 2 Ask pupils to try to recall the story from the previous reading. Use the experience as a basis for talking about oral transmission of myth.	Plurals: revise -s plurals and explain rules about -f/-ves plurals. Re-read second part of story, noting plurals. Exercise on -s and -f/ves plurals and exceptions.	1: Reading Comprehension, parts C & D. 2 & 3*: Reading Comprehension, parts A & D. 4: Reading Comprehension, part C (& B if time allows).	Pupils from Groups 2 & 3 present their reading of the story, followed by whole-class discussion based on part C of the Reading Comprehension sheet.
HOUR 3 Re-read 'Pandora's Box'. Discuss story from Pandora's point of view.	Revise use of 1st person for personal letters and 3rd person for narratives. Look at letter-writing conventions.	1–4: All groups write letter from Pandora to a friend, using 1st person. *Teacher supports Groups 2 & 3 as necessary.	Selected pupils read out their letters. Discuss: how do they compare with and reflect details in story?

RESOURCES

Photocopiable pages 85 ('Pandora's Box'), 86 (Reading Comprehension) and 87 (Plurals), board or flip chart, OHP and acetate (optional), writing materials (including evelopes – optional).

PREPARATION

Prepare at least one set of photocopiable pages 85 ('Pandora's Box'), 86 (Reading Comprehension) and 87 (Plurals) for each pair of children.

It may be useful to make an OHT of the story text as a focus for whole-class discussion throughout the unit, and also an OHT of photocopiable page 87 (Plurals) for use in the whole-class skills work for Hour 2.

Introduction

Explain to the children that the story they are going to read is a well-known Greek myth. A myth is a story which tries to explain something we don't understand or how something came into being – in this case, how pain and sorrow came into the world. Myths usually involve the actions or intervention of supernatural beings called gods and goddesses.

Next, read the story on photocopiable page 85 to the children. Pause at the point where Pandora has been given the box (before the asterisks). Discuss what might be in the box. Then finish the story and discuss how accurate the children's predictions were.

Whole-class skills work

Give out copies of the story and use it as a basis for the revision of grammar and punctuation skills covered so far, for example capital letters, nouns, adjectives, verbs, types of sentence, paragraphs, punctuation of speech, possessive apostrophe. This can be done in an informal question and answer session. Also, show how difficult words, such as Greek names, can be read more easily by breaking them down into syllables: Her-mes, Pan-dor-a, E-pi-me-the-us. Use the children's names to reinforce this skill further.

Differentiated group activities

The Reading Comprehension exercise on photocopiable page 86 contains a variety of tasks, which different groups should complete according to ability.
1*: Support this group in working through parts A and B.
2 & 3: Work independently on parts B and C.
4*: The teacher works with this group on part A.

Conclusion

Divide the story into three parts and ask each of Groups 1, 2 and 3 to do a reading presentation. Spend some time discussing their presentation.

Introduction

Ask the children how much of the story they can remember from the previous reading. Explain that, because myths were often told and passed on orally from one generation to another before they were eventually written down, there are often several versions of the same myth. And often, what started out as a short story ended up being extremely long. The most amazing example is a poem called 'The Odyssey' which ended up thousands of lines long when it was eventually written down!

Whole-class skills work

Ask the children to follow the story of 'Pandora's Box' on their copy as you re-read the second part, from 'Pandora gasped.' Draw their attention to the plurals in the text. Give out at least one copy of photocopiable page 87 (Plurals), between two children, and use it to revise -s plurals and to initiate teaching about -f/-ves plurals. The sheet can then be completed as a whole-class exercise, with the children working in pairs to fill in their sheets.

Differentiated group activities

The groups continue working on the Reading Comprehension exercise on photocopiable page 86 as follows:
1: Complete parts C and D (part D contains extension questions of a more challenging nature).
2 & 3*: Complete parts A and D supported by the teacher.
4: Complete part C, moving on to B if time allows. (Choose a small section of the story for them to prepare if they can move on to part B.)

Conclusion

Lead a whole-class discussion based on parts C and D of the Reading Comprehension exercise.

Introduction

Display the story of 'Pandora's Box' and read it through again with the children, asking them to think about the character of Pandora. What sort of person is she? How does she behave? What are her feelings about the events in the story?

Whole-class skills work

Now focus on how the story is written (in the 3rd person). Identify pronouns and verbs in the story that indicate the 3rd person. Then ask: how would the pronouns and verbs need to change if the story events were written as a letter from Pandora to her friend? Identify the differences between texts written in the 1st and 3rd person, for example I went, he/she/they went. Explain to the children that narratives are usually written in the 3rd person, while the 1st person is used for letters.

Move on to look at basic letter-writing conventions, including the address, date and so on. Write the start of a letter from Pandora to her friend in which she describes the events of the story from her point of view. Ask the children to help you compose the opening paragraph, and emphasize how this is being written in the 1st person, from Pandora's own viewpoint.

Differentiated group activities

All groups work on writing their own version of a letter from Pandora to her friend.
1: This group should be encouraged to give a detailed account of Pandora's thoughts and feelings, about events before and after opening the box, using the correct letter format, including paragraphs.
2 & 3*: As above, but with teacher support.
4: Encourage this group to focus on one main event, for example the arrival of Epimetheus with the box or opening the box. They can continue the letter started in the whole-class skills session if necessary. The use of paragraphs can be omitted to keep the task simple.

Conclusion

Ask selected children to read out their letters. Evaluate how well the letters reflect the story events and Pandora's character. Recap on the differences between 1st-person letters and 3rd-person narratives.

FURTHER IDEAS

The following unit 'Myth-maker' provides lesson plans in which the children write their own myths using a set of stimulus story cards to help them.

FOLLOW-UP (1 HOUR)

See page 205 which provides a grid plan for a 1-hour follow-up unit looking at and comparing other versions of 'Pandora's Box.'

# PANDORA'S BOX

A long time ago, when the world was new, there was no pain and no sorrow. Epimetheus lived happily in Ancient Greece with his beautiful wife, Pandora.

One day, they saw the god Hermes coming towards them. He was carrying a large, ornate, wooden box. It seemed very heavy.

'What's in that box?' asked Pandora.

'I can't tell you,' replied Hermes, 'but may I leave it here until I return?'

'Of course,' said Epimetheus. 'It will be safe in our house.'

Hermes thanked the couple and put the box in a corner, warning them, 'Whatever happens, do not open the box!'

'We won't!' promised Epimetheus and Pandora together. Hermes set off on his journey.

Pandora longed to know what was in the box. Day after day she looked at it, trying to guess what might be inside. Was it gleaming, gold coins or sparkling jewels? Or maybe bottles of sweet-smelling perfume, or fine silken clothes? Her curiosity was growing every minute.

Finally, Pandora could bear the suspense no longer. 'What harm could come if I take just one little peep?' she thought. Slowly she untied the gold cord around the box and began to lift the lid.

'Don't!' shouted Epimetheus, who was just coming into the room.

But it was too late. The lid was open.

* * * * * * *

Pandora gasped. There was no gold or jewels or perfume or silk inside the box, just a mass of ugly brown elves! And before she could shut the lid, out they swarmed. They spread their wings and buzzed around her like flies. They stung her arms and face, and they stung Epimetheus too! They were all the unpleasant things of the world that had been trapped inside.

Pandora slammed the lid shut. For the first time she felt pain and sadness. Epimetheus also had a new feeling – anger.

'You shouldn't have opened that box!' he shouted.

'You would have done it, if I hadn't done it first,' cried Pandora.

They shouted and quarrelled, and felt hurt and angry. And outside they could hear a sound they had never heard before. Other people were quarrelling, too!

'Oh, what have I done!' sobbed Pandora.

Then she heard a sweet little voice calling her name. It seem to come from inside the box.

'Release me! Let me out!' called the voice. 'I can help you.'

Pandora hesitated, but then opened the box again. Out flew a beautiful white creature with silver wings.

'Who are you?' asked Pandora.

'My name is Hope,' said the creature, 'and I can help the world to bear all the sorrows you have just let out.'

Then she healed Pandora's and Epimetheus' hurts, and went out into the world to do the same for all mankind.

READING COMPREHENSION

PART A

Find these words in the story. What do they mean? Use a dictionary to find out the meaning of any words you are not sure of.

ornate	longed	curiosity	bear
suspense	swarm	release	creature

PART B

In your group, prepare the story text for reading aloud to the rest of the class. You could do this by:

- marking all punctuation in red
- underlining words you will emphasize
- marking out who will read each section.

PART C

In your group, talk about the answers to the questions below. Then write your answers in full sentences in your book or on a separate piece of paper.

1. Who left the box at Pandora's house?
2. Why did he leave the box?
3. Why did Pandora want to open the box?
4. What did she hope to find?

PART D

In your group, talk about the answers to the questions below. Then write your answers in full sentences in your book or on a separate piece of paper.

1. Give some examples of the 'unpleasant things of the world'.
2. What pains and sorrows have you ever felt? Try to describe them.
3. Do you think this story is a good explanation of how pain and sorrow came into the world? Give reasons for your answer.

PLURALS

Remember: Most words form their plural by adding -s or -es.
Many words ending in -y change to -ies in the plural.

Write the plurals of these words.

Singular (one)	Plural (more than one)
house	
coin	
cry	
bottle	

Singular (one)	Plural (more than one)
cord	
box	
voice	
fly	

Rule: Many nouns ending in a single -f change of -ves in the plural.

Singular (one)	Plural (more than one)
elf	elves
loaf	loaves

Some common exceptions are:

Singular (one)	Plural (more than one)
dwarf	dwarfs
roof	roofs
chief	chiefs

Write the plurals of the words below. Be careful – not all the plurals end in ves!

Singular (one)	Plural (more than one)
wolf	
leaf	
cliff	
half	

Singular (one)	Plural (more than one)
roof	
thief	
calf	
wharf	

MYTH-MAKERS

OBJECTIVES

UNIT	SPELLING/VOCABULARY	GRAMMAR/PUNCTUATION	COMPREHENSION/ COMPOSITION
WRITING FICTION Writing myths using stimulus story cards: Myth-makers.	Break down long words into syllables. Use synonyms of 'said'.	Revise and extend writing of dialogue.	Apply story writing skills learned in 'Pandora's Box' unit, but with more imaginative content. Use a planning grid.

ORGANIZATION (3 HOURS)

	INTRODUCTION	WHOLE-CLASS SKILLS WORK	DIFFERENTIATED GROUP ACTIVITIES	CONCLUSION
HOUR 1	Introduce the oral myth-making activity using 'Myth-maker' story cards on photocopiable pages 91–94. Give tips for oral presentation.	Teach spelling by syllables. Apply the principles to pronouncing and spelling the long Greek names on the story cards.	1–4: All groups play the 'Myth-maker' card game and tell their orally-composed stories to each other. *The teacher works with Groups 1 & 4.	One pupil from each group is chosen to tell his/her oral story to the whole class.
HOUR 2	Display the Story Planner on photocopiable page 95.	Use the Story Planner photocopiable sheet to write a plan for the oral story.	1–4: Pupils in all groups begin to turn their myth into a written story. *The teacher works with Groups 2 & 3.	Examples of promising story beginning are read out.
HOUR 3	Display 'Pandora's Box' story on photocopiable page 85 and draw attention to the way the dialogue is handled.	Revise and develop writing and punctuating speech. Explore synonyms of 'said'.	1–4: Pupils in all groups finish the first draft of their stories. *The teacher works with Group 4.	Selected pupils read out first drafts of their story.

RESOURCES

Photocopiable pages 91–94 (Myth-maker Cards 1–4), 95 (Story Planner), 96 (Synonyms of 'Said') and 85 ('Pandora's Box' story – from the previous unit), OHP and acetate (optional), some sturdy card, laminator or sticky-backed plastic, scissors.

PREPARATION

Prepare at least one set of photocopiable pages 95 (Story Planner) and 96 (Synonyms of 'Said') for each pair of children. In addition, prepare an OHT of both these sheets, or enlarge them to A3 size. Do the same with the 'Pandora's Box' story from the previous unit as a focus for whole-class discussion in Hour 3. Photocopiable pages 91–94 (Myth-maker Cards 1–4) should be printed onto card, laminated and cut into sets, for at least one set per group.

Introduction

The main aim of this unit is to revise and build on the key writing skills introduced in the 'Beat the Bully' unit on pages 33–42. The Myth-maker cards act as a stimulus for ideas, the whole-class skills sessions provide revision of key skills, and the Story Planner is a reminder of the story structure developed in 'Beat the Bully'.

Begin by arranging the class into groups of four or five, broadly within their ability groups, but overlapping where necessary to create groups of the required size. Then model the oral myth-making activity using the set of cards prepared from photocopiable pages 91–94. The 'Gods' and 'Monsters' cards are drawn directly from Greek mythology; the 'Objects' and 'Places' cards are less specific so that the children do not feel bound to retell known stories. Explain that the cards can be used to make myths or legends. Demonstrate the procedure by taking one group of children through the following process while the others watch:

■ Shuffle each set of cards ('Gods', 'Monsters', 'Objects' and 'Places') separately and place the sets face down in the middle of the table.
■ The first player takes the top card from each set and places them face up in front of her.
■ The player must make up an oral story using all the cards (the teacher should do this during the demonstration session).
■ Continue the game clockwise around the table.
■ When everyone has had a turn, decide whose was the best story.
■ The rest of the group should then help that person to prepare the story for presentation to the class or other groups.

Whole-class skills work

Revise how to tackle the spelling and pronunciation of long words by breaking them down into syllables. Give 'February' as an example. Explain to the children that, if it is pronounced correctly and broken into its four syllables, it is easier to spell: *'Feb-ru-ar-y'*.

Read out the words below for the children to try out. Tell them to work in pairs. They should begin by repeating the words slowly to each other, trying to hear the separate syllables, then they should try to write them down:

■ remember
■ appearance
■ completely
■ description
■ disappear
■ instalment.

Next, help the children to pronounce the Greek names on the cards by breaking them down into syllables.

Differentiated group activities

1–4: All groups play the Myth-makers card game and tell their orally-composed stories to each other. *The teacher works with Groups 1 and 4.

Conclusion

One child from each group is chosen to tell his/her oral story to the whole class. The rest of the class should listen carefully and positive comment should be invited, for example by asking the class: 'What did you like about that story?'

Introduction

Explain that the oral stories from Hour 1 are now going to be developed into written stories. Remind the children that the first key skill is planning a story with an effective structure: a good beginning, middle and end. Display photocopiable page 95 (Story Planner) on an OHP or as an A3 enlargement, and go through the different sections. Remind the children how this structure applied to 'Beat the Bully' and how it could apply to some of the oral stories they heard the day before.

Whole-class skills work

Now give a copy of the Story Planner photocopiable sheet to all the children. Remind them that the boxes in the planner are to help them write a structured story with a beginning, middle and end. Group 1 should be encouraged to adapt the structure freely, or to write a plan in a completely different way, if they wish. Group 2 should be encouraged to follow the basic structure, but should write several paragraphs in each section. Group 4 should follow the planner closely, writing one paragraph for each section. Explain to all the children that they can develop or change their oral stories in any way, and can borrow ideas from the stories they heard at the end of Hour 1.

Differentiated group activities

1–4: All groups begin to turn their myth into a written story.
*The teacher works with Groups 2 and 3, with a particular focus on the key skills being revised and developed in this unit (see 'Objectives').

Conclusion

Good examples of beginnings written by children in Groups 2 and 3 are read out to the class. Other children are invited to say what they liked about them. The teacher comments on effective features and encourages other children to use them.

HOUR 3

Introduction

Display an OHT of the 'Pandora's Box' story on photocopiable page 85 and use it to point out the punctuation and layout of dialogue. The attention of more able children should be drawn to the indentations made for each change of speaker. Teach them the rule: every time the speaker changes, start a new line and indent.

Whole-class skills work

Display an OHT or an A3 enlargement of photocopiable page 96 (Synonyms of 'Said'). Either do the entire cloze exercise as a whole-class activity, or do some of it with the whole class and let pairs finish it off, coming back together to share and evaluate responses. The children can use the list at the bottom of the page, add to it and then use it later as a reference to support their writing.

Differentiated group activities

1–4: All groups finish the first draft of their stories.
*The teacher works with Group 4.

Conclusion

Selected children from all groups read out their first draft, followed by discussion and suggestions for further revision from the teacher.

FOLLOW-UP (1 HOUR)

See page 206 which provides a grid plan for a 1-hour follow-up unit which enables the 'myth' stories to be finished off and 'published' in a class collection of myths and legends.

MYTH-MAKER CARDS 1

Gods & Goddesses	Gods & Goddesses	Gods & Goddesses

HERA	APOLLO	POSEIDON
Gods & Goddesses	Gods & Goddesses	Gods & Goddesses

ARTEMIS	APHRODITE	ARES
Gods & Goddesses	Gods & Goddesses	Gods & Goddesses

ATHENE	ZEUS	HERMES

MYTH-MAKER CARDS 2

Monsters

HYDRA

Monsters

MINOTAUR

Monsters

HARPY

Monsters

SIREN

Monsters

CYCLOPS

Monsters

CHIMERA

Monsters

GORGON

Monsters

SPHINX

Monsters

CERBERUS

MYTH-MAKER CARDS 1

Gods & Goddesses	Gods & Goddesses	Gods & Goddesses

ARES	HERA	APHRODITE
Gods & Goddesses	Gods & Goddesses	Gods & Goddesses

POSEIDON	HERMES	APOLLO
Gods & Goddesses	Gods & Goddesses	Gods & Goddesses

ATHENE	ZEUS	ARTEMIS

MYTH-MAKER CARDS 2

Monsters

CERBERUS

Monsters

MINOTAUR

Monsters

HARPY

Monsters

HYDRA

Monsters

CYCLOPS

Monsters

SPHINX

Monsters

GORGON

Monsters

CHIMERA

Monsters

SIREN

MYTH-MAKER CARDS 3

Objects

GOLD

Objects

SWORD

Objects

MAGIC ROBE

Objects

CHARIOT

Objects

STATUE

Objects

CROWN

Objects

SHIP

Objects

LYRE

Objects

WHIRLPOOL

MYTH-MAKER CARDS 4

Places	Places	Places
LABYRINTH	ORACLE	TEMPLE
CITADEL	MAGIC ISLAND	MEDITERRANEAN SEA
CAVE	UNDERWORLD	PALACE

STORY PLANNER

■ Use this grid to plan your new story.

Beginning	Describe a character or place.
Middle	Describe a place or character.
	Describe a problem.
	Describe attempts to solve the problem.
End	Say how the problem is solved.

SYNONYMS OF 'SAID'

The word 'said' is often used in stories, but sometimes it can be replaced by a *synonym* (a word with a similar meaning) which is more accurate.

For example: 'You're standing on my toe!' *said* Tim.
would be better as: 'You're standing on my toe!' *yelled* Tim.

Below is part of the text from a myth. Work with a partner to fill in the blanks with synonyms of 'said'. A list of synonyms is given at the bottom of the page to help you, but you can, of course, think of your own!

Ariadne took Theseus to the mouth of a dark cave. 'This is the entrance to the

labyrinth,' she _____. 'You will find the minotaur in there.'

    'What is he like?' _____ Theseus.

    'Terrible!' _____ Ariadne. 'He is half man, half bull, and has the

strength of ten men!'

    'Then how shall I kill him?' _____ Theseus.

    'Take this sword,' _____ Ariadne.

    Ariadne gave Theseus a magnificent bronze sword with an edge as keen as a razor.

    'This must be worth a fortune!' he _____.

    'It is my father's and is the best sword in the kingdom,' she _____

proudly.

    Theseus still hesitated.

    'And if I do kill the minotaur, how shall I find my way out?'

    'With this,' _____ Ariadne.

    She gave him a ball of twine.

    'Fasten one end here and unwind it as you go,' she _____, 'then all

you have to do is follow it out.'

    'If I'm still alive…' _____ Theseus.

Synonyms of 'said': replied, answered, moaned, asked, questioned, remarked, repeated, queried, shouted, snapped, whispered, grumbled, screamed, muttered, yelled, called, sighed, complained, declared, agreed, cried, begged, offered, pleaded, announced, remarked, joked, groaned, enquired, exclaimed, suggested, whined, warned, smiled.

JASON AND THE GOLDEN LYRE

OBJECTIVES

UNIT	SPELLING/VOCABULARY	GRAMMAR/PUNCTUATION	COMPREHENSION/ COMPOSITION
REDRAFTING SIMULATION 'Jason and the Golden Lyre'.	Identify misspelled words in own and others' writing.	Revise and consolidate grammar and punctuation skills.	Learn skills of redrafting through a simulation.

ORGANIZATION (2 HOURS)

	INTRODUCTION	WHOLE-CLASS SKILLS WORK	DIFFERENTIATED GROUP ACTIVITIES	CONCLUSION
HOUR 1	Read and discuss the first draft of story when using the Myth-maker cards from previous unit.	Examine the text of their story and discuss teacher's comments written on it.	1–4*: All pupils work on a copy of the text, redrafting aspects highlighted by teacher, according to their ability.	Selected pupils read out their improvements and story endings to the whole class.
HOUR 2	Use a 'real' first draft written by one of the pupils as the basis for suggesting redrafting for improvement.	Use as a basis for oral revision of key skills.	1–4*: Pupils work in pairs to help each other revise their own stories.	Discuss how the stories have been improved. Read out some examples of these improvements.

RESOURCES

Photocopiable page 99 ('Jason and the Golden Lyre'), each child will need the first draft of a story which they have written (for Hour 2), OHP and acetate (optional), writing materials.

PREPARATION

If possible, prepare photocopiable page 99 as an OHT or enlarge to at least A3 size. In addition, make enough copies of this sheet for one between two children.

Introduction

This unit is effective as a stand-alone study of redrafting, but has been designed to follow on from the 'Myth-makers' unit. The main objective is to teach the children how to redraft content, as well as spelling and punctuation in *context*. Explain that 'Jason and the Golden Lyre' (photocopiable page 99) is the first draft of a child's story written using the Myth-makers cards from the previous unit. (If that unit has not been done previously, just present the story as a first draft of a myth.) Read the story, then re-read it. Discuss the content, in particular:

■ Is the opening effective? How could traditional story language be used to help identify the story as a myth?

■ How could the description be improved, in particular the character descriptions of Jason and the Gorgon?

■ What would be a good way to end the story?

Whole-class skills work

Explain to the children that, when they are writing, they have to keep an eye on all the different skills involved. Tell them that they need to keep revisiting what they have written and ask themselves: How can I improve this so that the reader fully understands and enjoys what I have written? Display the OHT or A3 enlargement of the 'Jason and the Golden Lyre' story. Discuss the teacher's comments written on this photocopiable sheet and use them as a basis for oral revision of key skills, focusing on two or three aspects of grammar and/or punctuation that you feel your class needs to revise.

Differentiated group activities

Give out copies of photocopiable page 99, one between two children. All the children should work on redrafting the piece according to the teacher's comments included as part of the sheet, with support from the teacher as necessary. Emphasize that the children should pay attention to spelling, grammar and punctuation as part of the redrafting process. The level of this task will be determined by the teacher according to the children's ability. For example:
1*: Encourage the children to write a final draft, using both the teacher's comment on the sheet as well as their own initiative to enhance the story in any way that occurs to them.
2 & 3*: These two groups could be expected to show reasonable proficiency in responding to most of the teacher's comments on the sheet.
4*: This group are likely to need more teacher support. Make improving the detail and description the main priority with this group.

The children can write in the spaces provided on the sheet or on a separate sheet of paper if they need more space.

Conclusion

Selected children read out their improvements and endings to the whole class. Discuss the effectiveness of these improvements in comparison to the original, and decide which endings are the most effective and why. Conclude by emphasizing that effective redrafting involves exploring ways to make the telling of the story better and more interesting, as well as identifying punctuation, grammar and spelling errors.

Introduction

In this session, the redrafting 'simulation' is translated into the context of the children's own work. Choose a 'real' first draft written by one of the children (with his/her permission, of course!) and read it out. Discuss possible improvements to the content.

Whole-class skills work

Revise the key skills which were the focus of the drafting in Hour 1 and ask the children to write the following text in their notebooks as a reminder:
   You can improve your stories by:
■ adding more detail to descriptions of character and place
■ using carefully-chosen adjectives to improve description
■ paragraphing correctly
■ punctuating dialogue correctly
■ accuracy in spelling.

Differentiated group activities

1–4*: All the children should work on redrafting stories they have started previously. Let them work in pairs to help each other revise their stories. Ask them to exchange stories. First they should play 'teacher' and mark the work with positive suggestions as in the 'Jason and the Golden Lyre' photocopiable sheet. (It might be useful to display this sheet as a source of reference.) Then they should take back their own stories and try to revise their work as suggested. Emphasize that they should go through the redrafting process every time they write to try to make their work as effective as possible, before handing it in for the teacher's marking and comments.

Conclusion

Discuss how the stories have been improved. Read out examples of improvement. Then sum up the purpose of the exercise by emphasizing that a similar process should be applied to all written work.

JASON AND THE GOLDEN LYRE

Jason was a nice boy, but he was very poor.

(Write a longer description of Jason. Find a better adjective than 'nice'.)

He worked hard all day, but never seemed to have any money. He desided that he would try to make his fortune.

(What was his job? Describe what was hard about it.)

He had heard that there was a cave in the mountans.

(What should you do to show that you have started a new paragraph?)

In the cave was a lyre.

(Think of a good adjective to describe the lyre.)

The legend said that anyone who played the lyre would make the beutiful music in the world and woud become rich and famous. He said goodbye to his parents and set out on his journey. After a few days he came to the mountan. It was huge.

(Write a more vivid description of the mountain.)

After a long search he found the cave. Outside, an old man was sitting.

I would not go in there if I was you, she said.

Why not? said Jason.

(Insert speech marks!)

Because there is a Gorgon in there! One glance from it's eyes will turn you to stone!

(Take out the incorrect apostrophe. Add some description to make the Gorgon sound more terrible.)

Jason thought for a moment, but decided he would risk it rather than be poor all his life. He went nervusly into the cave. It was very dark and he felt frightend.

(Say more about how Jason felt to make it more exciting.)

Soon he couldnt see anything at all, so he felt his way forward with his hands.

(Put in the missing apostrophe.)

At last he saw a golden glow in the distance. It must be the lyre he thought.

Well done so far. Now, in addition to the comments made above, you need to:

1. Check spellings. There are 6 mistakes. Find them and correct them.

2. Check grammar and punctuation. There are 5 mistakes (in addition to those already pointed out on the sheet), including a missing word.

3. Finish the story. Does Jason meet the Gorgon? Who wins the fight? Does he find the golden lyre? Does it make him rich and famous?

BOOK TOKEN

OBJECTIVES

UNIT	SPELLING/VOCABULARY	GRAMMAR/PUNCTUATION	COMPREHENSION/ COMPOSITION
READING NON-FICTION Persuasion: Book Token.	Develop vocabulary from reading.	Revise present and past tenses. Understand person/verb agreement.	Develop basic reading skills. Identify and understand features of persuasive writing.

ORGANIZATION (2 HOURS)

	INTRODUCTION	WHOLE-CLASS SKILLS WORK	DIFFERENTIATED GROUP ACTIVITIES	CONCLUSION
HOUR 1	Display the advertisement on photocopiable page 102 and read with the class. Discuss features of persuasive writing.	Identify difficult vocabulary in text and establish meaning.	1: Complete all parts of Reading Comprehension sheet. 2 & 3*: Complete all parts of Reading Comprehension sheet with teacher support. 4: Complete parts A & C of Reading Comprehension sheet.	Pupils share responses to selected literal questions from Reading Comprehension sheet.
HOUR 2	Re-read the advertisement. Pupils share responses to selected evaluative questions from Reading Comprehension sheet.	Revise present tense. Understand agreement of person/verb.	1*: Write a similar advertisement. 2 & 3: As above, but concentrate on main text and illustrations only. 4*: As for Groups 2 & 3 but with teacher support.	Selected pupils from each group share their advertisements. Evaluate how effective they are as persuasive writing.

RESOURCES

Photocopiable pages 102 (Book Token Advert) and 103 (Reading Comprehension), board or flip chart, OHP and acetate (optional), dictionaries, writing materials.

PREPARATION

Make enough copies of pages 102 and 103 for one between two children. If possible, prepare an OHT or A3 enlargement of page 102 (Book Token Advert) as a focal point for discussion.

Introduction

Display the advertisement on photocopiable page 102 as an OHT or A3 enlargement. Read the main part of the advertisement (the rhyme). Then re-read it with the class joining in. Establish that the text is an advertisement and that the purpose of it is to persuade people to buy or to do something. Read the smaller text at the bottom of the advertisement. What is this advertisement trying to persuade us to do? (Buy a Book Token as a Christmas present.) How does it do this? (It uses rhyme, language and pictures that create images; it addresses the reader directly and tells them what the benefits are for her/him; it uses the present tense; it uses the imperative verb form.)

Whole-class skills work

The advertisement contains some words and phrases that may be unfamiliar to the children (see next page). Explore the meanings of these in this session in a variety of ways, including direct teaching, inferring from the context, using a dictionary and so on. Here are some of the words and phrases you will probably need to explore:

- carcass – a dead body, in this case, the remains of the turkey
- whacked – a slang expression meaning 'tired out'
- 'look on the bright side' – a well-known saying meaning 'think about the good things'
- courtesy – kind behaviour
- Book Token – a trademark of the company that sells Book Tokens. A trade mark is protected by law so that nobody else can use it.

Differentiated group activities

All groups work on the Reading Comprehension sheet on page 103 at the appropriate level:
1: Complete all sections A, B and C.
2 & 3*: As above, with teacher support.
4: Complete sections A and C.

Conclusion

Choose a selection of the literal comprehension questions from the Reading Comprehension sheet and invite the children to share their responses.

Introduction

Re-read the advertisement on photocopiable page 102. Remind the class how the pictures and words are working together to create a certain effect. Share some of the responses to the evaluative questions from the Reading Comprehension sheet.

Whole-class skills work

Use the advertisement text to revise the present tense and person/verb agreement. Ask the children how the first two lines of the poem in the advertisement would read if written out as a prose instead – for example 'When Christmas is over and the last cracker is cracked.' Then ask the children what 'turkey's' is short for in the next line ('turkey is'). Write the present tense of the verb 'to be' on the board or flip chart:

	SINGULAR	PLURAL
1st person:	I am	We are
2nd person:	You are	You are
3rd person:	He/she/it is	They are

Discuss singular and plural persons and the need to use the correct verbs with them. Ask the children to find other examples of present tense verbs in the passage. Are they singular or plural?

Differentiated group activities

All groups write an advertisement at their own level, based on the Book Token model.
1*: Write a similarly structured advertisement for a product of the children's own choice. The children should follow the format of the advertisement including linking in illustrations, although the text doesn't have to rhyme. Encourage them to write additional small print at the bottom of the advertisement as in the model. They could also design a trade mark for their product.
2 & 3: As for Group 1, but concentrate just on the main copy and linking illustrations.
4*: As for Groups 2 and 3, but with teacher support.

Conclusion

Ask selected children from each group to share their advertisements with everyone else. Evaluate how effective they are as persuasive writing, emphasizing the features identified in Hour 1.

FURTHER IDEAS

Ask the children to make a collection of advertisements for homework. Use their contributions to make a wall display and discuss the different uses of language, how pictures are used, how persuasive they are and so on.

When Christmas is over, the last cracker cracked,

The turkey's a carcass and don't you feel whacked,

Pine needles are falling, the kids' toys are broken,

Look on the bright side you still have a Book Token.

You still have a treat in store for a cold day in January.

You can walk into a bookshop and enjoy the thrill of buying books with someone else's money.

You'll find your eyes looking at your favourite story books, and even those expensive hardback books!

Enjoy it, courtesy of Book Tokens Ltd and the person who gave you one for a present.

Remember, *after* Christmas only comes but once a year.

BOOK TOKENS

READING COMPREHENSION

PART A

1. Pick out the rhyming words in the advertisement. Why do you think the advertiser decided to use rhyme?

2. The advertisement describes three things that make us feel sad when Christmas is over. What are they?

3. How do the pictures add to this message?

PART B

1. The small print at the bottom of the advertisement tells us three things we can look forward to if we have a Book Token. What are they?

2. The last line is based on a well-known saying. What is the saying and how has it been adapted for this advertisement?

3. Do you think this advertisement is effective – does it persuade you that a Book Token is a good Christmas present?

PART C

1. Do you think a Book Token is a good present? Would you like to receive a Book Token for Christmas.

2. If you had a Book Token now, what would you spend it on?

RULES RULE!

OBJECTIVES

UNIT	SPELLING/VOCABULARY	GRAMMAR/PUNCTUATION	COMPREHENSION/ COMPOSITION
WRITING NON-FICTION Persuasion: Rules Rule!	Explore Greek and Latin prefixes.	Revise the imperative verb form.	Write a set of rules. Justify the rules.

ORGANIZATION (2 HOURS)

	INTRODUCTION	WHOLE-CLASS SKILLS WORK	DIFFERENTIATED GROUP ACTIVITIES	CONCLUSION
HOUR 1	Display the Megacoaster rules on photocopiable page 106 as an OHT or A3 enlargement.	Briefly discuss the need for rules. Ask questions to test understanding.	1–4*: All groups discuss a set of rules for their class. Remind them that they need to have a reason for each one.	Groups 2 & 3 share ideas arising during the discussion.
HOUR 2	Display the Class Rules template on photocopiable page 107 as a model for writing, and explain how to use it.	Use the word 'megacoaster' as a starting point for the exploration of common Greek and Latin prefixes. Revise the imperative verb form.	1*: Write a set of rules for the class, giving reasons for each one. 2 & 3: As above, but using the photocopiable template as a model. 4*: As above, writing on the template. The teacher supports the group in guided writing.	Groups 1 & 4 share some of their work with the class.

RESOURCES

Photocopiable pages 106 (Welcome to Megacoaster), 107 (Greek and Latin Prefixes) and 108 (Class Rules), board or flip chart, OHP and acetate (optional), writing materials.

PREPARATION

Prepare OHTs of all photocopiable pages. Alternatively, enlarge them to A3 size. In addition, prepare one copy of photocopiable page 108 (Class Rules) for each child in Group 4.

Introduction

Display the Megacoaster rules on photocopiable page 106 as an OHT or A3 enlargement and read them to the class. Briefly discuss the need for rules. Ask what could go wrong if there were no safety rules for riding on a roller-coaster. Where else are rules needed? Test the children's understanding of the Megacoaster Rules by asking questions, for example:

■ You are seven years old. You have a cheeseburger in one hand and a cola drink in the other. What must you do to be allowed on the ride?
■ Will you be allowed on the ride by yourself?
■ Will your five-year-old sister be allowed on the ride if you go with her?

Whole-class skills work

Explain that many words are made up from small parts of old languages, particularly Ancient Latin and Greek. From these languages, we have taken a range of prefixes which, interestingly, are used to make up some of our newest words: 'Megacoaster' is a good example. Ask the children to guess how this word has been made up and what its two parts mean (*mega* = very big, 'coaster' = from 'roller coaster').

The children can then explore this further using the Greek and Latin Prefixes photocopiable page 107. Read through the sheet with them and explain how to play the game (instructions are on the sheet). Take them through a few examples to get them started, if necessary. Although the prefixes sound hard, the game is easy, and the children will enjoy playing it as a class or in pairs. When the game is over, point out to the children that many new words are formed in exactly the same way.

Differentiated group activities

1–4*: Explain to the children that rules for a classroom are also very important and that this is their chance to have a say in the rules of their own classroom. Tell them that the best rules from all the groups will be put together to make a poster and that these will be the rules for the class. Ask each group to discuss what would be a good set of rules for this. Remind them that they need to have a good reason for each rule. The teacher should spend some time helping each group.

Conclusion

Groups 2 and 3 share their ideas with the whole class, and the teacher uses their ideas as the basis of a general discussion. Give particular emphasis to the need for a good reason for each rule.

Introduction

Display an OHT of the Class Rules template on photocopiable page 108 and explain how each group should use it when they come to complete the sheet a little later on. Group 1 should adapt the basic pattern freely: each paragraph states a rule and gives reasons for the rule. Groups 2 and 3 should follow the template closely, but should give more than one reason where they can. Group 4 should write on the template itself (each child in this group will therefore need their own copy of this sheet).

Whole-class skills work

Revise the imperative verb form. Remind the children that this is the basic form of the verb: 'pull' in rule 4 and 'follow' in rule 7 are the clearest examples in the 'Welcome to Megacoaster' text on photocopiable page 106. Ask the children to brainstorm a number of simple rules or instructions beginning with an imperative verb. These should be collected on the board or flip chart and briefly discussed.

Differentiated group activities

1*: Write an essay which gives a list of class rules supported with reasons.
2 & 3: As above, but using the template as a model.
4*: As above, but writing on the template. The teacher supports the group in guided writing.

Conclusion

Groups 1 and 4 share some of their work with the class.

FURTHER IDEA

Select the most appropriate of the collection of rules and make them into a class poster. The class then works to this agreed set of rules. The children could be asked to research other sets of rules, as part of their homework. These could be made into a display. Don't forget to include the most famous set of rules of all – the ten commandments!

WELCOME TO MEAGACOASTER

THE FASTEST ROLLER-COASTER IN THE COUNTRY!

For your safety, please follow these rules:

- Children under 5 are not allowed on this ride.

- Children under 9 must be accompanied by an adult.

- No food or drinks are allowed on this ride.

- When you are seated, pull the safety-bar down over your shoulders.

- Do not reach out from the car.

- Do not leave the car until it has come to a complete stop.

- Follow the instructions of the attendant at all times.

Enjoy your ride!

GREEK AND LATIN PREFIXES

PREFIX	MEANING	LANGUAGE	EXAMPLE	MEANING
anti-	opposite/ against	Greek	antidote	something that works *against* a poison
bio-	life	Greek	biography	the story of a *life*
hyper-	over	Greek	hypermarket	a very large supermarket
mega-	large	Greek	megalosarus	a *large* dinosaur
micro-	small	Latin	microscope	an instrument for looking at very *small* objects
maxi-	the most	Latin	maximum	*the most*
multi-	many	Latin	multiplex cinema	a cinema with *many* screens
ultra-	beyond	Latin	ultraviolet	a colour *beyond* violet
super-	more than	Latin	supermarket	*more than* an ordinary market
techno-	technical	Greek	technology	the study of machines and other *technical* things
tele-	over a distance	Greek	television	those pictures have come *over a distance*

Play the Prefix Game with a partner

- Think of a noun, for example teacher, book, car, television, computer and so on.
- Your partner chooses a prefix from the list.
- Put your prefix and noun together, for example teleteacher, technobook, microcar.
- Write a dictionary definition for your new word, for example: 'A teleteacher teaches you on television while you stay at home.'

Now swap places and repeat the game.

CLASS RULES

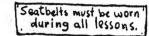

Rules for behaviour in class are important because

After our discussion, I think that these four rules are most important:

Rule 1 "_____."

This rule is important because

Rule 2 "_____."

This rule will help by

Rule 3 "_____."

This rule is important because

Rule 4 "_____."

This rule will help by

I put the rules in this order because

ALPHABETICAL ORDER

OBJECTIVES

UNIT	SPELLING/VOCABULARY	GRAMMAR/PUNCTUATION	COMPREHENSION/ COMPOSITION
REFERENCE AND RESEARCH SKILLS Alphabetical order.	Learn vocabulary for common reference books. Understand how dictionaries and thesauri can help with developing vocabulary.		Understand the purpose of alphabetical order. Practise using alphabetical order.

ORGANIZATION (1 HOUR)

	INTRODUCTION	WHOLE-CLASS SKILLS WORK	DIFFERENTIATED GROUP ACTIVITIES	CONCLUSION
HOUR 1	Identify reference books for different purposes. Understand that reference books, such as dictionaries, telephone books etc are organized in alphabetical order.	Oral practice of alphabetical order. Recognize that the alphabet can be divided into three parts to help with finding information.	1*: Practise finding words in dictionary. Complete the 'Alphabetical Order' photocopiable sheet. 2 & 3: Complete parts A & B of the photocopiable sheet, and part C if time allows. 4*: Complete part A independently, and part B with teacher support.	Play the Human Alphabet Game.

RESOURCES

Examples of reference books that use alphabetical order: a dictionary, a thesaurus, an encyclopaedia, a telephone book with yellow pages; board or flip chart, class dictionaries, photocopiable page 111 (Alphabetical Order), paper, writing materials.

PREPARATION

Collect examples of the reference books listed above. Make enough copies of photocopiable page 111 for each child. Prepare alphabet words for the Human Alphabet game outlined in the 'Conclusion' section below. Start by choosing two words, one beginning with *A* and one beginning with *Z*. Write each word in large letters on a separate piece of paper. Then, depending on the number of children in the class, write other words, at least one beginning with each of the rest of the letters of the alphabet. Write these on separate pieces of paper, enough for one each for the remaining children.

Introduction

Draw the children's attention to the collection of alphabetical reference books (see 'Resources'). Ask them to identify what each one is. Then ask questions such as:
■ I need to ring a plumber because I have a leaky tap. Where should I look?
■ I don't know the meaning of the word 'innovate'. How can I find out?
■ I want to know about the different types of dinosaur. Which book will tell me?
■ Where can I find some other words to use instead of 'said'?
    Then ask: What else do I need to know besides which book to use? Establish the

for knowledge of alphabetical order because it helps us to find information in reference books, and in libraries, which are also arranged alphabetically.

Whole-class skills work

Begin this session with a rapid question and answer quiz testing the children's knowledge of alphabetical order. For example:
- What letter comes after *g*?
- What letter comes before *m*?
- What is the fifth letter?
- Which letter comes between *r* and *t*?
- Which letters are on either side of *e*?
- Which letter is the second to last?

Then explain that in addition to knowing letter order, it is helpful to know which part of the alphabet a letter is in. Dividing the alphabet into three parts means that we can open a reference book, such as a dictionary to roughly the right spot, rather than having to go through it from front to back. Write on the board or flip chart:

The **front** of the book has words that begin with **A, B, C, D, E, F, G, H**.
The **middle** of the book has words that begin with **I, J, K, L, M, N, O, P, Q**.
The **back** of the book has words that begin with **R, S, T, U, V, W, X, Y, Z**.

Then ask in which part of a reference book you would find, for example the words:

dinosaur, swim, McDonald, vegetable, computer, nice and so on.

Differentiated group activities

The children will each need a copy of the photocopiable page 111 (Alphabetical Order) for this session.
1*: Ask the children to find particular words in the dictionary as quickly as possible after you say them. Encourage them to build up speed in finding the correct page and then scanning the page for the correct word. They should then complete the photocopiable sheet independently.
2 & 3: Work on the photocopiable sheet, completing at least parts A and B, and C if they are able and time allows. The children could work in pairs to complete the exercise.
4*: Work on part A of the photocopiable sheet on their own or in pairs. Then complete part B with teacher support.

Conclusion

End the hour by playing the Human Alphabet Game, using the resources described in 'Preparation' above. Take the two words beginning with *A* and *Z*. Give one word each to two children. Then, depending on the number of children in the class, give out the other words beginning with each of the rest of the letters of the alphabet, handing out one word for each remaining child.

Tell the *A* and *Z* children to stand at the front of the room, one at each end, displaying their word. Ask the remaining children to look carefully at their words and then organize themselves between the two other children in alphabetical order. Discuss any problems that occur. For example, if two children have words beginning with the same letter, they will need to look at the second letter of the word.

To increase the difficulty of this activity, introduce a time element, either by setting a time limit, or timing it and getting the children to try to improve the next time they try the activity.

FURTHER IDEA

The children could compile a list of all the names in their class and put these in alphabetical order, perhaps making one list for first names and another for surnames. These lists could form part of an 'Alphabetical Order' class display. Alternatively, the children could work in pairs or small groups to arrange a pile of class or library fiction books in alphabetical order, using the authors' names and/or the titles. A competitive element can be added if appropriate by measuring the time that each group takes to complete the task.

ALPHABETICAL ORDER

PART A
Write each group of words in alphabetical order.

water	_____	fist	_____	under	_____
mountain	_____	horse	_____	yellow	_____
plastic	_____	idea	_____	ghost	_____
answer	_____	money	_____	honest	_____
anchor	_____	balloon	_____	record	_____
child	_____	draw	_____	elephant	_____

PART B
Write each group of words in alphabetical order. Be careful – for words that begin with the same letter you must look at the second letter!

piano	_____	lemon	_____	scarf	_____
drum	_____	banana	_____	sweater	_____
violin	_____	plum	_____	skirt	_____
cello	_____	lime	_____	sock	_____
flute	_____	peach	_____	sleeve	_____
clarinet	_____	orange	_____	shirt	_____

PART C
In which part of a dictionary would you find the words below? Write each word on the chart under **Front**, **Middle** or **Back**.

crow	winter	fun	jar	dinner	lace
basket	scale	river	tiger	yell	pattern
team	food	song	anger	home	game
important	need	vest	pudding	laugh	left

Front	Middle	Back

SONG OF THE ANIMAL WORLD

OBJECTIVES

UNIT	SPELLING/VOCABULARY	GRAMMAR/PUNCTUATION	COMPREHENSION/ COMPOSITION
READING POETRY Cultural variety: 'Song of the Animal Word' – a traditional Pygmy song.	Explore words that imitate sounds. Look at words with silent letters.	Mark up a text for reading aloud with intonation and expression.	Respond orally to a Pygmy song. Understand how layout aids meaning.

ORGANIZATION (2 HOURS)

	INTRODUCTION	WHOLE-CLASS SKILLS WORK	DIFFERENTIATED GROUP ACTIVITIES	CONCLUSION
HOUR 1	Shared reading of the 'Song of the Animal World' poem on photocopiable page 115. Discuss layout.	Explore words that imitate sounds. Explain how to mark up text for reading aloud with expression.	1 & 4*: Develop a choral reading of poem. 2 & 3: Work on words on the Animal Noises photocopiable sheet (page 116).	Groups 2 & 3 share some of their invented sound words. Groups 1 & 4 present their choral reading.
HOUR 2	Re-read poem.	Explore words with silent letters.	1: Work on the Silent Letters Words photocopiable sheet (page 117). 2 & 3*: Develop a choral reading of the poem. 4: Work on the Silent Letter Words photocopiable sheet (page 117).	Groups 1 & 4 share answers to work on silent letters. Groups 2 & 3 present their choral readings.

RESOURCES

Photocopiable pages 115 ('Song of the Animal World'), 116 (Animal Noises) and 117 (Silent Letter Words), board or flip chart, OHP and acetate (optional), a range of simple percussion instruments, dictionaries, writing materials.

PREPARATION

Make enough copies of photocopiable page 115 ('Song of the Animal World' poem) for each child in the class. Ideally, also reproduce the poem as an OHT, or enlarge it to A3 size. Make enough copies of photocopiable page 116 (Animal Noises) for Groups 2 and 3. Make enough copies of photocopiable page 117 (Silent Letter Words) for each child in Group 1 and for pairs in Group 4.

Introduction

'Song of the Animal World' is a traditional Pygmy song which was chanted to the accompaniment of drums. Explain to the children that Pygmies are an African race of people who are very small. Just as with myths and legends, songs like this were passed on by word of mouth for thousands of years before they were written down.

Give out copies of the poem and, if possible, display it on an OHP or as an A3 enlargement on the board. Then read the poem while the children follow the text.

Explain the terms 'solo' and 'chorus' and show how the poem is written in the form of a script, with 'solo' parts for a narrator, fish, bird and monkey, and the 'chorus' chanting the sound words. Emphasize that this is a poem meant for dramatic presentation and so the way in which it is read aloud is especially important.

Now demonstrate how to mark up a text for reading aloud with intonation and expression. For example, the children could:

- underline or highlight their own part
- double underline words which must be emphasized
- add notes such as 'loudly', 'angrily' and so on.

Explain that in their groups, they will be preparing a performance of the poem.

Whole-class skills work

Draw the children's attention to the sound words in the poem. What does the fish say? How do the bird and monkey go? What other words do they know that imitate the sound of an object or action? Brainstorm some 'sound' words, writing them up on the board or flip chart (for example: *buzz, hiss, bang, snap*). Point out that sometimes we want to write sounds or nonsense words for which there is no 'standard' spelling. In this case, we spell phonetically, as in the poem: Hip! Viss! If you wish, introduce the children to the grammatical term for sound words: onomatopoeia. It's an excellent Greek word for breaking down into syllables!

narrator

Solo (narrator):

The fish goes...
The bird goes...
The monkey goes...

pause for chorus each time

Chorus: Hip!
Viss!
Gnan!

Solo (fish):
(with actions)

I jump to the left,
I turn to the right,
I'm being the fish
That slip through the water, that slips,
That twists and springs!

Solo (narrator):

Everything lives, everything dances,
everything chirps...
The fish...
The bird...
The monkey...

get louder

Solo (bird):
(with actions)

The bird flies away,
Flies, flies, flies,
Goes, comes back, passes,
Rises, floats, swoops,
I'm being the bird.

Hip!
Viss!
Gnan!

Solo (narrator):

Everything lives, everything dances,
everything chirps...
The fish...
The bird...
The monkey...

Hip!
Viss!
Gnan!

Solo (monkey):
(with actions)

The monkey—from branch to branch
He runs, hops, jumps,
With his wife and his brat,
His mouth stuffed full, his tail in the air,
Here's the monkey, here's the monkey!

Solo (narrator):

Everything lives, everything dances,
everything chirps...
The fish...
The bird...
The monkey...

Hip!
Viss!
Gnan!

Differentiated group activities

1 & 4*: Children in these groups combine to develop a choral reading of the poem. Mix the two groups together and subdivide them into groups of four so each child can have a part. If larger groups are necessary, children without a part could be given percussion instruments to try to recreate the style of the Pygmy original. Each group prepares a dramatic presentation of the poem. Encourage movement and improvisation where action is required. The teacher gives support to all groups as necessary.

2 & 3: All children in these groups work on photocopiable page 116 (Animal Noises) to explore sound words further.

Conclusion

Select children from Groups 2 and 3 to share some of the sound words they collected. Then ask Groups 1 and 4 to perform their choral readings. If time does not allow all sub-groups to present their poems in this session, then use the Introduction to Hour 2 for doing this.

Introduction

If any sub-groups from Hour 1 have not performed their reading of the poem, they should do so now. Display the poem again and this time, divide the whole class into parts for reading the poem aloud. Act like a conductor and orchestrate the reading, bringing in the groups as they need to speak and indicating when they should be loud or soft, fast or slow.

Whole-class skills work

Draw the children's attention to the word 'Gnan!' How did they pronounce it? They may have said 'ga-nan' – but did any of them notice that it was like the words 'gnat' and 'gnaw' in the English language? How are these words pronounced? Explain that there are many English words that have 'silent' letters. These letters are not pronounced but must be written, so they are tricky to spell!

Write *gn-* on the board or flip chart, and 'gnat' and 'gnaw' underneath it. Can the children think of any other words containing the letter combinati *-gn*? (For example: *gnome, gnu, sign*). Which letter is silent? Now write 'knit' and 'wrap' on the board. Read the words and determine which are the silent letters. Brainstorm some other examples.

Differentiated group activities

1: Work individually to complete photocopiable page 117 (Silent Letter Words).
2 & 3*: As for Groups 1 and 4 in Hour 1.
4: Work in pairs to complete the Silent Letter Words photocopiable sheet, filling in boxes selected by the teacher.

Conclusion

Select members of Groups 1 and 4 to share some of the silent letter words they have collected. Then ask sub-groups of Groups 2 and 3 to perform their choral readings.

FURTHER IDEA

Groups could develop one of the following improvisations based on the pattern of 'Song of the Animal World':
■ Song of the Human World
■ Song of the Machine World
■ Song of the Dinosaur World
■ The Silent Song of the Undersea World.

SONG OF THE ANIMAL WORLD

Solo (narrator):   The fish goes...   **Chorus:**   **Hip!**
                     The bird goes...   **Viss!**
                     The monkey goes...   **Gnan!**

Solo (fish):   I jump to the left,
(with actions)   I turn to the right,
                     I'm being the fish
                     That slip through the water, that slips,
                     That twists and springs!

Solo (narrator):   Everything lives, everything dances, everything chirps...
                     The fish...   **Hip!**
                     The bird...   **Viss!**
                     The monkey...   **Gnan!**

Solo (bird):   The bird flies away,
(with actions)   Flies, flies, flies,
                     Goes, comes back, passes,
                     Rises, floats, swoops,
                     I'm being the bird.

Solo (narrator):   Everything lives, everything dances, everything chirps...
                     The fish...   **Hip!**
                     The bird...   **Viss!**
                     The monkey...   **Gnan!**

Solo (monkey):   The monkey—from branch to branch
(with actions)   He runs, hops, jumps,
                     With his wife and his brat,
                     His mouth stuffed full, his tail in the air.
                     Here's the monkey, here's the monkey!

Solo (narrator):   Everything lives, everything dances, everything chirps...
                     The fish...   **Hip!**
                     The bird...   **Viss!**
                     The monkey...   **Gnan!**

Traditional Pygmy Song

ANIMAL NOISES

Different animals make different noises. Write the noise words for each of the animals below. Choose from the words given:

woof	oink	baa	miaow	moo	cluck	hiss	buzz

sheep _____   dog _____

snake _____   bee _____

hen _____   cat _____

pig _____   cow _____

Now write the noise words for each of these animals. If you are not sure how to spell the word, try it phonetically first. Then look it up in the dictionary to check.

horse _____   duck _____

owl _____   bird _____

wolf _____   mouse _____

goose _____   lion _____

Think up an imaginary animal. Give it a name and make up a noise word for how it sounds!

Gorp!

SILENT LETTER WORDS

Some words have silent letters in them. You don't pronounce these letters when you say the word, but they must be there when you write the word! You can find some examples of words like this in the boxes below. Add in as many others as you can for each box. Remember, the silent letters can be at the beginning, in the middle or at the end of the word!

b as in lamb doubt	**h as in** hour rhyme	**n as in** autumn
g as in gnome	**k as in** knee	**t as in** castle
gh as in bright	**l as in** talk	**w as in** wrong who

p is also a silent letter when it comes before *n*, *s* and *t* at the beginning of a word as in 'pterodactyl'. Find out what that word means!

ANIMAL ALPHABET

OBJECTIVES

UNIT	SPELLING/VOCABULARY	GRAMMAR/PUNCTUATION	COMPREHENSION/ COMPOSITION
WRITING POETRY 'Animal Alphabet' by Zoe Goodall.	Know alphabetical order. Revise vowels and consonants.	Know when to use capital letters.	Use the alphabet as a pattern for writing a free-verse poem. Understand the term 'alliteration' and use the device in writing.

ORGANIZATION (2 HOURS)

	INTRODUCTION	WHOLE-CLASS SKILLS WORK	DIFFERENTIATED GROUP ACTIVITIES	CONCLUSION
HOUR 1	Share the 'Animal Alphabet' poem on photocopiable page 121 and discuss features of its pattern.	Revise alphabetical order and vowels and consonants.	1 & 2: Write their own alphabet poem. 3 & 4*: Write another version of 'Animal Alphabet' using the prepared sheet to provide the structure.	Selected pupils present their poems to the class.
HOUR 2	Use a popular chant as a pattern for writing. Practise alphabetical order and alliteration.	Teach the term 'alliteration' and examine the poem for examples. Revise the uses of capital letters.	1–4*: All groups work on verses for a class poem. The teacher supports all groups at their level.	Share selected verses and evaluate. As a group, come up with a format for publication.

RESOURCES

Photocopiable page 121 ('Animal Alphabet'), simple dictionaries, board or flip chart, OHP and acetate (optional), a book of names and their meanings, plus an atlas (both are optional), writing materials.

PREPARATION

Make enough copies of the poem on photocopiable page 121 for one between two children. If possible, make an OHT as well. In addition, make a copy of the poem and delete everything but the animal names. Make enough copies of this for each child in Groups 3 and 4.

Introduction

Read the 'Animal Alphabet' poem with the class and tell them that the poet is a child of their age. Discuss some of the key points: What is the theme? (Zoo animals.) What is the structure? (It is based on the order of the alphabet. Almost all lines end with 'at you'. The introduction has been repeated at the end, which rounds off the poem effectively. Point out also how the poet has tackled the problem of the 'difficult' letters of the alphabet.)

Whole-class skills work

Use the poem as a basis for revising alphabetical order. This can be done in a quick-fire question and answer session, for example: Which letter comes after *g*? Which letter comes before *s*? Where would you find *d*? Is *w* in the beginning, middle or end of the alphabet? Which word comes first in alphabetical order – *mother* or *nephew*?

Now explain the term 'alliteration' (two or more words which are next to or close to

each other and which begin with the same sound). Revise the terms 'vowels' and 'consonants' and explain that the strongest effects with alliteration are achieved with consonants. Ask the children to underline some examples in 'Animal Alphabet'. Remind them of their previous work on acrostic poems and explain that a dictionary is helpful in looking for words which begin with a particular letter.

Finally, point out that the usual convention for poetry writing is that each new line begins with a capital letter.

Differentiated group activities

1 & 2: Write their own alphabet poems. Encourage them to use alliteration. Here are some suggested subjects if they need a starting point:

■ *An Alphabet of my Dislikes*
■ *A Christmas Alphabet*
■ *An Alphabet of People I Know*
■ *An Alphabet for a Small Child* (use the pattern: 'A is for ...').

3 & 4*: Write another version of 'Animal Alphabet' using the photocopiable poem from which everything but the animal names have been deleted (see 'Preparation' above). The teacher should give support where needed, particularly to less able children. If necessary, the use of the photocopiable sheet to provide a structure for the poem can be restricted to Group 4.

Conclusion

Select some children from each group to present their poems to the class. The rest of the class should evaluate by saying what they liked about the poems. In particular, they could comment on the use of alliteration, and how effectively the writer has dealt with the 'difficult' letters of the alphabet.

Introduction

Write the following poem beginning on the board or flip chart:

> A my name is Ashrah
> And my friend's name is Alan.
> We come from Aberdeen
> And we like apples.
>
> B my name is Ben
> And my friend's name is Betty.
> We come from Birmingham
> And we like basketball.

Discuss the pattern (the verses are in alphabetical order; each verse uses names, places and objects beginning with the appropriate letter). With the children, write a couple of other verses, using names of children in the class. Then try adding appropriate adjectives to achieve alliteration. For example:

> C my name is charming Charlie
> And my friend's name is cute Cathy.
> We come from cold Cardiff
> And we like chilly churches.

Whole-class skills work

Revise what capital letters are used for – to begin a sentence, to begin a new line of poetry, for people's names, for places, for the days of the week, for the months of the year, for special days. Ask the children for examples of each and write them on the board. Then write some sentences on the board without capital letters. Ask the children

to put in the capital letters where needed. For example:
- mary had a little lamb/whose fleece was white as snow.
- mr. jones lives in london with his cat called flossie.
- tuesday is valentine's day.

Differentiated group activities

1–4*: All groups should write verses for an alphabet book based on the above model. Give each group a section of the alphabet to work on. For example, Group 4 could work on A–D, Group 3 on E–J, Group 2 on K–Q, and Group 1 on R–Z. If available, a book of names and an atlas may prove useful for the more difficult letters! Work with all groups to help them extend their ideas and ensure appropriate capitalisation.

Conclusion

Share some of the verses and evaluate them. Discuss how the verses might be put together to create the class alphabet book, or how they could be used as part of a display, perhaps. Agree on a format and at some later time, allow the children to compile their work.

FURTHER IDEA

Find examples of alliteration in newspaper headlines and advertisements. Cut them out and make a wall display. Ask the children to make up some of their own alliterative headlines and advertising slogans. Add them to the display. Think of more examples of well-known sayings which use alliteration. Write them out and add them to the display.

ANIMAL ALPHABET

You go to a zoo
To look at the animals,
But they're all looking at you!

Antelopes stare at you,
Baboons and bullocks glare at you,
Cats and cobras look at you as if to say 'Silly Moo'!
Dogs and dingoes howl at you,
Elephants spray water at you,
Fish blow bubbles at you,
Gorillas growl and roar at you,
Hippopotamuses yawn at you,
Insects hum and buzz at you,
Jaguars snarl and hiss at you,
Koala bears smile at you,
Lions are so proud they just ignore you,
Monkeys laugh and make faces at you,
Newts splash and wriggle at you,
Octopi wave their arms at you,
Parrots hurl abuse at you,
Quails flutter and flap at you,
Rattlesnakes bare their fangs at you,
Seals call and clap at you,
Tarantulas creep menacingly towards you,
Unicorns puzzle you (because you thought they didn't exist!)
Venomous snakes spit at you,
Whales spout at you
X....(this creature's name is a secret!)
Yaks moo at you,
Zoo-keepers keep their eye on you.

You go to a zoo
To look at the animals,
But they're all looking at you!

Zoe Goodall

HOW TO MAKE A PAPER AEROPLANE

OBJECTIVES

UNIT	SPELLING/VOCABULARY	GRAMMAR/PUNCTUATION	COMPREHENSION/ COMPOSITION
READING NON-FICTION Procedural genre: How to make a Paper Aeroplane.	Read, understand and spell appropriate language for subject matter. Understand abbreviations.	Use and understand the imperative verb form. Understand the need for concise writing.	Read and understand instructions.

ORGANIZATION (1 HOUR)

	INTRODUCTION	WHOLE-CLASS SKILLS WORK	DIFFERENTIATED GROUP ACTIVITIES	CONCLUSION
HOUR 1	Explain to the class that they are going to make a paper aeroplane following the written instructions on photocopiable page 124.	Explain the imperative form of the verb using examples that they will meet in the aeroplane instructions.	1 & 2: Make a paper aeroplane using the text-only version of photocopiable page 124. 3 & 4*: As above, but using the illustration version of photocopiable page 124.	Evaluate the aeroplanes and the two versions of the instructions.

RESOURCES

Photocopiable page 124 (How to Make a Paper Aeroplane), writing materials, rulers.

PREPARATION

Make enough copies of photocopiable page 124 (How to Make a Paper Aeroplane) as it stands for one between two children in Groups 3 and 4. Now use some paper to mask off the diagrams in the right-hand column of the sheet so that only the text is showing. Make enough copies for one between two children in Groups 1 and 2.

Introduction

Brainstorm situations in which it is important to follow oral or written directions, for example what to do in case of a fire, how to get from one place to another, how to play a game, how to make or use something.

Think of a game most of the children are familiar with and tell them that you are going to write the 'how-to-play' instructions on the board as they tell them to you. Write them out in a continuous paragraph exactly as they say them. Then analyse what you have written. Is it clear and concise? What could be done to improve the text? Establish the features of good instructions:

■ State clearly what you are going to explain.
■ State clearly what preparation is needed (items to collect, ingredients/utensils to gather and so on).
■ Tell the steps in order.
■ Include all the essential information, leaving out any details that are not necessary.
■ Use pictures/diagrams to help.

Explain to the class that, in their groups, they are going to make a paper aeroplane following some written instructions. At the end of the lesson, they will evaluate both the aeroplanes and the instructions. Explain that they may notice that different groups have different instructions, but that this is part of the evaluation. Give out the text-only instructions prepared for Groups 1 and 2, and the instructions which include diagrams to Groups 3 and 4.

Whole-class skills work

Explain that because instructions tell us what to do, the sentences are written as orders or commands (imperatives), for example *fold, measure, make*. Refer to the first two instructions on the photocopiable sheet as examples and then ask the children to find all the other imperative verbs. What do they notice about where they are in the sentence? Instructions usually begin with the verb, although sometimes words indicating sequence are used (*first, then, next, finally* and so on), and the subject ('you') is implied.

Differentiated group activities

All groups use photocopiable page 124 (How to Make a Paper Aeroplane), with the sheet adapted for Groups 1 and 2 (see 'Preparation') to omit the illustrations.
1 & 2: Make a paper aeroplane using the text-only version of the instructions.
3 & 4*: As above, but using the full version of the sheet which includes diagrams.
The children try out their aeroplanes and evaluate how well they fly.

Conclusion

Evaluate the instructions. Were they clear and easy to follow? Were all the necessary steps included – and in the correct sequence? Was there anything in them that should have been left out? Discuss whether the instructions containing the diagrams were more helpful. End the lesson by summing up on key features of instructions (procedural writing).

FURTHER IDEAS

Ask the children to write a similar set of instructions for a procedure that they know, such as making a cup of tea.

FOLLOW-UP (1 HOUR)

See page 207 which provides a grid plan for a 1-hour follow-up unit on reading procedural texts.

HOW TO MAKE A PAPER AEROPLANE

What you need
A sheet of A4 paper,
a pencil, a ruler.

What to do

1 Take a sheet of A4 paper, fold in half (longways), then flatten out again.

2 Fold over the top left-hand corner at 45 degrees.

3 Fold over the top right-hand corner at 45 degrees.

4 Fold in half again.

5 Measure and rule a line 3cm up from the fold.

6 Fold the wings outwards.

7 Make two 1cm tears at the end of the wing folds.

8 Bend the flaps at the ends of the wings down slightly.

9 Try your aeroplane. Launch it gently.
Do not throw.

10 Adjust the flaps for a better flight.
If the plane swoops up too steeply, bend the flaps down.
If it goes down too steeply, bend the flaps up.

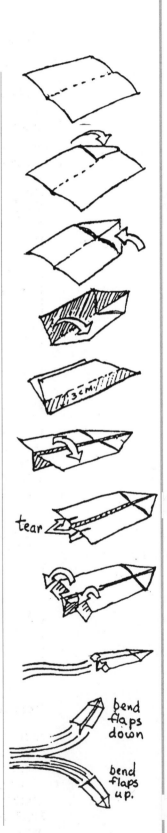

PARTY TIME!

OBJECTIVES

UNIT	SPELLING/VOCABULARY	GRAMMAR/PUNCTUATION	COMPREHENSION/ COMPOSITION
READING NON-FICTION Procedural genre: Party Time!	Spell words by syllables. Use and spell correctly appropriate vocabulary for procedural writing.	Use imperative verb form.	Write clear instructions for a variety of purposes. Use features of procedural genre.

ORGANIZATION (2 HOURS)

	INTRODUCTION	WHOLE-CLASS SKILLS WORK	DIFFERENTIATED GROUP ACTIVITIES	CONCLUSION
HOUR 1	Establish party theme by looking at various objects and kinds of writing associated with parties. Distinguish procedural writing in party planning.	Use text of How to Make a Paper Aeroplane on page 124 to revise the layout and language of procedural writing.	All groups broadly plan own party. 1: Half the group write a recipe; the other half write some party game instructions. Reciprocal evaluation. 2: In pairs, half the group write some party decoration instructions; the other half write some directions on how to get to party from a given point. Reciprocal evaluation. 3*: As for 2 above, but with teacher support. 4*: Work in pairs, writing instructions on how to play a party game.	Share ideas for party themes. Select pupils from Groups 1 & 4 to share their work. Selected pairs in Groups 2 & 3 share their work.
HOUR 2	Select pupils from Groups 2 & 3 to share their work from Hour 1. Emphasize good examples, and revise the features of procedural writing as necessary.	Brainstorm imperative verbs. Work on spelling longer words by syllables.	1*: Half the group write some party decoration instructions; the other half write some directions on how to get to a party from a given point. Reciprocal evaluation. 2*: In pairs, half the group write party game instructions; the other half write recipe instructions. Reciprocal evaluation. 3: Work in pairs, writing recipe instructions. 4: Work in pairs, writing instructions on how to get to a party from a given point.	The class votes for the best party theme, recipe, decoration and game.

RESOURCES

A collection of a variety of objects and examples of writing associated with parties (for example a guest list, a shopping list, an invitation, a party hat, a party decoration, instructions on how to play a party game, a party recipe, directions showing how to get to the party, a party balloon with message on and so on) – just enough to give the children a clue about the theme of this unit, photocopiable page 124 (How to Make a Paper Aeroplane) from the previous unit, board or flip chart, OHP and acetate (optional), writing materials.

PREPARATION

Collect a variety of party objects and examples of writing as listed above. If possible, prepare an OHT of photocopiable page 124 (How to Make a Paper Aeroplane).

Introduction

Show the children the various party objects you have collected, but don't make any reference to parties. Ask if they can guess what the objects have in common. When you've established the party theme, use the objects to discuss what's involved in planning a party. Point out that although parties are fun, they require a lot of work to organize! Look at the examples of writing and establish those which are procedural and those which are not (the lists and invitation are not). How can the children tell? Make a list of the things involved in a party that require procedural writing, for example:

■ how to play a party game
■ how to make a party recipe
■ how to make a party decoration
■ how to get to the party.

Briefly brainstorm different types of party and suggest that a themed party is a good way to link all the elements of it. Explain that in their groups, they are going to plan a themed party, deciding what and who the party is for, where it will be held and what the theme will be. They will then write instructions for the items listed above.

Whole-class skills work

Display an OHT of How to Make a Paper Aeroplane on photocopiable page 124. Remind the children that writing directions and instructions requires 'command' or 'order' sentences using the imperative or direct action verb. Ask the children to pick out the imperative verbs on the OHT and then to brainstorm a list of imperative verbs that would be useful in writing directions and instructions, for example *take, turn, go, hide, move, sit, pass, cut, paste, colour, mix, bake, slice* and so on.

Differentiated group activities

All groups subdivide into threes or fours and decide what and who their party is for, where it will be held and what the theme will be. Remember that games, food and decorations should be linked to the theme. Encourage the children to be creative about game and recipe names!

1: Half the children write recipe instructions and half write instructions on how to play a party game. Half-way through the session, swap with a partner and read and evaluate each other's work.

2: Working in pairs, half the children write instructions on how to make a party decoration and half write directions on how to get to the party from a given point. As above, swap with another pair half-way through session.

3*: As for Group 2, but with teacher support.

4*: Working in pairs, write instructions on how to play a party game.

Conclusion

Share the groups' various ideas for party themes. Select children from Groups 1 and 4 to share their work.

Introduction

Select pairs of children from Groups 2 and 3 to share their work from Hour 1. Encourage others to follow good examples, and revise any features of procedural writing that the children need to.

Whole-class skills work

Ask if anyone can spell 'invitation'. Write it on the board as they spell it. Explain that for longer words, breaking them down into syllables helps with spelling. Check that all the children understand the word 'syllable'. Clap out the syllables in 'invitation' and write the word up on the board again in syllables: *in-vi-ta-tion*. (If the original spelling was incorrect, point this out and correct it.)

Emphasize to the children that syllabic spelling is useful but it is necessary that they pronounce words correctly and clearly. Many long words can be spelled easily and phonetically when this method is used (provided the children are familiar with some common spelling patterns such as -*tion*, -*able* and so on). Ask the children to spell these other words by the syllabic method:

some-bo-dy
re-mem-ber
dis-as-ter
dic-tion-ar-y
ar-gu-ment
Feb-ru-a-ry
si-mi-lar
in-struc-tions.

Differentiated group activities

1*: Half the children write instructions on how to make a party decoration and half write directions on how to get to the party from a given point. Halfway through the session, swap with a partner and read and evaluate each other's work.
2*: Working in pairs, half the children write instructions on how to play a party game and half write recipe instructions. As above, swap with another pair halfway through the session.
3: Working in pairs, write recipe instructions.
4: Working in pairs, write instructions on how to get to the party from a given point.

Conclusion

Selected pairs in Groups 2 and 3 share their work. Finally, ask the class to vote for the best party theme, recipe, decoration and game.

BREAKFAST BITES

OBJECTIVES

UNIT	SPELLING/VOCABULARY	GRAMMAR/PUNCTUATION	COMPREHENSION/ COMPOSITION
READING NON-FICTION Packaging: 'Breakfast Bites'.	Explore opposites. Recognize how the suffixes -ful and -less influence word meaning.	Investigate the grammar of media text and slogans. Explore the use of capital letters in media texts. Identify essential words in sentences. Identify adjectives.	Read and discuss media texts. Explore ways of conveying ideas in a shortened form. Compare and contrast similar idea.

ORGANIZATION (2 HOURS)

	INTRODUCTION	WHOLE-CLASS SKILLS WORK	DIFFERENTIATED GROUP ACTIVITIES	CONCLUSION
HOUR 1	Look at/read the different sections of the 'Breakfast Bites' pack on photocopiable pages 130–131. Identify and examine the different features.	Grammar of media text and slogans – omission of verbs and/or nouns. Use of capital letters for emphasis.	1–4*: Read and discuss 'Breakfast Bites', based on parts A–C of the Reading Comprehension exercise on photocopiable page 132.	Share ideas from discussions.
HOUR 2	Examine the range of cereal packets.	Explore adjectives and their opposites.	1–4: Classify cereal packets using the comparison grid on photocopiable page 133. *The teacher supports Groups 1 & 4.	Share ideas from the classification exercise, and sum up on what makes an effective cereal packet.

RESOURCES

Photocopiable pages 130–131 (Breakfast Bites 1 and 2), 132 (Reading Comprehension) and 133 (Comparing Cereal Packets), a broad selection of cereal packets, board or flip chart, OHP and acetate (optional), writing materials.

PREPARATION

Well in advance of the activity in Hour 2, ask the children to bring in empty cereal packaging from home – but make sure you have enough for those who are unable to do this. Make enough copies of all the photocopiable pages for one between two. If possible, make OHTs or A3 enlargements of both the 'Breakfast Bites' photocopiable sheets. For more able children, prepare a few extra copies of photocopiable page 133.

Introduction

Ask how many children have had cereal for breakfast. Did they look at the cereal packet? Can they remember what was on it? Brainstorm a list of features typically found on cereal packaging and write them on the board or flip chart, for example:
- name of cereal
- slogan
- nutritional information
- special offers/free gifts
- sell by/best before date
- weight

- ingredients
- storage instructions
- manufacturer's name and address.

Now display the 'Breakfast Bites' sheets as OHTs or A3 enlargements and establish that they show the front, back and sides of a cereal box. Read the different sections of the 'Breakfast Bites' packaging. Begin with the front, asking the children what stands out the most (the brand name, the '10% EXTRA', and the picture of the cereal). Then read the back. Note that one side of the packet contains a special offer, and the other side, nutritional information. Match the features on the packaging with those in your list.

Whole-class skills work

Study the grammar of media texts and slogans by looking at some examples on the packet, for example:

- 'FULL OF WHOLEWHEAT GOODNESS'
- 'FREE PUZZLE INSIDE'.

Are these full sentences? What has been left out? How would they read if they were full sentences? What words are not essential to the reader's understanding of the text?

Investigate the use of capital letters on the 'Breakfast Bites' packet. For what different purposes are capital letters used? Draw the children's attention to the brand name 'Breakfast Bites' and explain the term 'brand name'. Say that brand names are often deliberately written in a particular style to try to make them memorable. Can the children think of brand names for other products that have a memorable image?

Differentiated group activities

1–4*: All groups work on the Reading Comprehension questions on photocopiable page 132 as follows:
1: Complete all parts of the exercise.
2 & 3: Complete as much of the sheet as they are able.
4: Concentrate on part A.
*The teacher supports each group as necessary, especially Group 4.

Conclusion

Discuss answers to the Reading Comprehension exercise. Remind the children to bring in a cereal packet for study the next day.

Introduction

Examine the cereal packets brought in by the children. Recap on the various features of packaging discussed in Hour 1. How many can the children identify in these packets? Explain that they will be studying and classifying the cereal packets later in the lesson.

Whole-class skills work

Remind the children of the meaning of the word 'adjective'. Ask them to find as many examples of adjectives as they can on the cereal packets. List them on the board, then challenge the children to find as many opposites as they can, for example *extra (less/fewer), slim (fat), new (old)*.

Talk about how some adjectives can be turned into their opposites by adding the prefix un- (*un/kind, un/necessary, un/usual, un/happy* and so on). Ask the class to brainstorm as many ideas as possible. Talk about how some adjectives that end with the suffix –ful can be made into their opposites by changing the ending to –less. Again, brainstorm examples – *hopeful/hopeless, careful/careless, useful/useless* and so on.

Differentiated group activities

1–4: All groups work on comparing the cereal packets and recording their notes on the chart on photocopiable page 133. Note that the tasks increase in difficulty, so differentiation can be provided by instructing each group how far down the sheet they should go. There is enough space on each sheet to compare two packets. This may be enough for children in Group 4, but encourage more able children to compare more packets by using additional sheets. *The teacher supports Groups 1 and 4 in this session.

Conclusion

Share ideas from the comparison exercise. What makes an effective cereal packet?

BREAKFAST BITES 1

10% EXTRA FREE

Cerealities

Breakfast Bites

Take a bite - Take a breakfast bite!

Breakfast Bites

Take a bite - Take a breakfast bite!

FULL OF WHOLEWHEAT GOODNESS FORTIFIED WITH EXTRA VITAMINS

Collect all 4 of our puzzles

FREE PUZZLE INSIDE

Full of Wholewheat Goodness

600g

BREAKFAST BITES 2

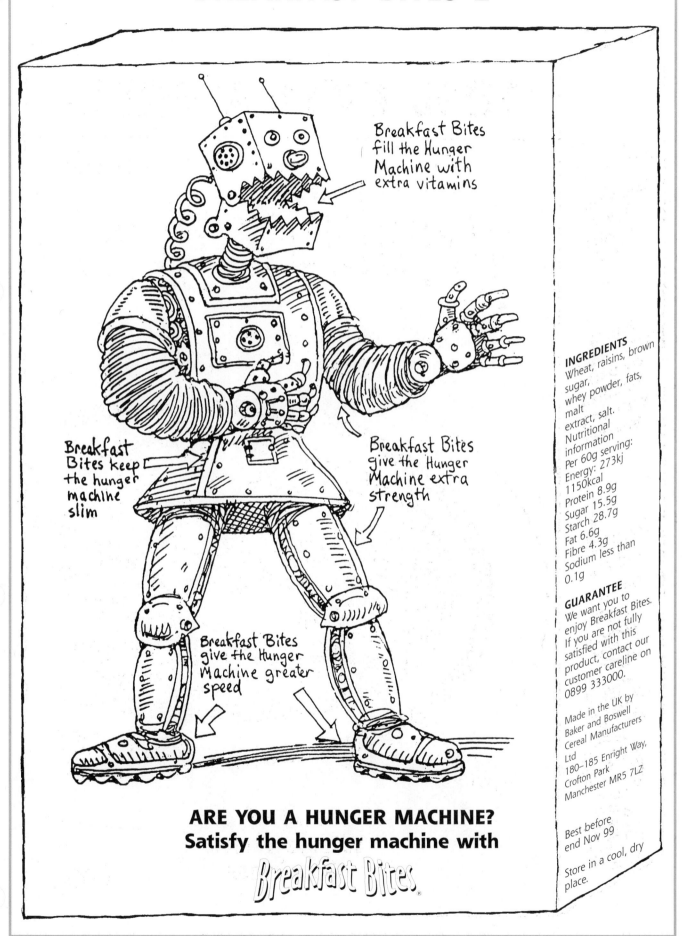

Breakfast Bites fill the Hunger Machine with extra vitamins

Breakfast Bites keep the hunger machine slim

Breakfast Bites give the Hunger Machine extra strength

Breakfast Bites give the Hunger Machine greater speed

ARE YOU A HUNGER MACHINE?
Satisfy the hunger machine with

Breakfast Bites

INGREDIENTS
Wheat, raisins, brown sugar, whey powder, fats, malt extract, salt.
Nutritional information
Per 60g serving:
Energy: 273kj 1150kcal
Protein 8.9g
Sugar 15.5g
Starch 28.7g
Fat 6.6g
Fibre 4.3g
Sodium less than 0.1g

GUARANTEE
We want you to enjoy Breakfast Bites. If you are not fully satisfied with this product, contact our customer careline on 0899 333000.

Made in the UK by Baker and Boswell Cereal Manufacturers Ltd
180–185 Enright Way, Crofton Park Manchester MR5 7LZ

Best before end Nov 99

Store in a cool, dry place.

READING COMPREHENSION

PART A

Look at the front of the packet and answer these questions:

- Which words stand out?
- Why do they stand out?
- What is there on the packet to persuade you to buy the cereal?
- What is the manufacturer's name?
- What is the brand name?
- Find two slogans and write them down.

PART B

Look at the back of the packet and answer these questions:

- Describe four ways in which 'Breakfast Bites' satisfy 'The Hunger Machine'.
- Find two more slogans on the back of the packet.
- Write out the slogans but add the missing words to make complete sentences.
- What else on the back of the packet may persuade you to buy the cereals?

PART C

Look at the sides of the packet and answer the questions below:

- Study the nutritional information. How could this persuade a health-conscious person to buy the product?
- The list of figures for nutrition looks impressive, but how do you know if these figures are good?
- What else on the sides of the packet might persuade you to buy the product?

COMPARING CEREAL PACKETS

BASIC INFORMATION Name of cereal Manufacturer Type of cereal Size of pack (in grams) Price		
SPECIAL OFFERS Free gifts, offers at a reduced price, discount coupons and so on.		
SLOGANS Write down two or three of the best slogans.		
BACK OF PACKET All sorts of things can be found here from board games to special offers. Describe what you find.		
SIDES OF PACKETS Describe briefly what is on each side. Also look at the top and bottom of the packet!		
NUTRITIONAL INFORMATION How much: Protein, Carbohydrate, Fat, Fibre What else is in it?		
MARKET Can you tell who this product is aimed at – children, adults, athletes and so on?		

CEREAL PACKET

OBJECTIVES

UNIT	SPELLING/VOCABULARY	GRAMMAR/PUNCTUATION	COMPREHENSION/COMPOSITION
WRITING NON-FICTION Packaging: Cereal packet.	Identify different ways of spelling the same sound 'sh', 'ee'.	Experiment with deleting and substituting adjectives and noting the effect on meaning. Use capital letters for different purposes. Explore how appropriate fonts help to convey meaning.	Explore ways of writing ideas and messages, in shortened forms for media texts.

ORGANIZATION (2 HOURS)

	INTRODUCTION	WHOLE-CLASS SKILLS WORK	DIFFERENTIATED GROUP ACTIVITIES	CONCLUSION
HOUR 1	Use the model from previous unit to demonstrate main design features of a cereal packet.	Study different typefaces and discuss the appropriateness of each one.	1–4*: All pupils plan their cereal packet and write a draft of all the slogans, promotional ideas and other text.	Share and evaluate ideas for cereal packets. Pupils display their designs. The class discusses which they would like to buy and why.
HOUR 2	Display some of the packets brought in my pupils and explain how they can use them as models for their own designs. Revise the grammar of slogans and packaging.	Identify different spellings of same sounds. Examine the appropriate use of adjectives and list alternatives.	1–4*: All pupils draw their cereal packet designs.	Discuss the effective use of shortened forms of writing.

RESOURCES

Photocopiable pages 130–131 (Breakfast Bites 1 and 2 from previous unit) and 136 (Typefaces), a selection of cereal packets, A4 drawing paper, coloured pencils/pens or paint and brushes, OHP and acetate (optional), thesauruses, writing materials.

PREPARATION

Well in advance of the activity, invite the children to bring in empty cereal packets from home if they have not already done so for Hour 2 of the previous unit. Make enough copies of pages 130 and 131 (Breakfast Bites 1 and 2) for one between two children (if they have not already been photocopied for the previous unit). Photocopiable page 136 (Typefaces) could also be prepared as an OHP transparency.

Introduction

Use photocopiable pages 130 and 131 (Breakfast Bites 1 and 2) to remind the children of the main design features of a cereal packet. What features on packaging provide the consumer with information about the product? What features are intended to persuade the shopper to buy the product? Talk about the ways in which information is conveyed.

Look at the photocopiable page 136 (Typefaces) and discuss which style of typeface is appropriate for which purpose, for example:

- Which typeface would be suitable for a rounded cereal that looked like bubbles?
- Which typeface would be suitable for a crunchy, crispy cereal?
- Which typeface would be suitable for a seriously healthy cereal?
- Which typeface would be suitable for a fun cereal?
- Which typeface would be suitable for a slogan?
- Which typeface would be suitable for the main text?

(Explain to the children that the term 'font' is often used instead of typeface – especially in computer terminology.)

Whole-class skills work

Ask the children to look at the cereal packet design sheets. How many words can they see that contain the sound *'sh'*? *(Nutritional, delicious, information, machine.)* Brainstorm lists of other words that follow the same spelling patterns. Next ask them to find as many words as they can with the sound *'ee'*. *(Wheat, free, machine.)* Think of other examples.

Differentiated group activities

1–4*: All groups work to plan and draft packaging text for their invented cereal product. The first task is for the children to think of the type of cereal they would like to sell and to invent a name for it. They can then plan their cereal packet and write a draft of all the slogans, promotional ideas and other text they wish to use. Children in Group 4 could concentrate on the front of the cereal box. Children in Group 1 should be expected to give attention to details such as 'sell by' dates, guarantees, storage instructions and so on. The teacher supports each group as appropriate.

Conclusion

Share ideas for cereals, names for cereals and promotional copy. If they have not already done so for the activity in the previous unit, ask the children to bring in a cereal packet which they would like to use as a model for their work in Hour 2.

Introduction

Display some of the cereal packets brought in by the children and explain how they can use them as models. Tell them that the best way to do this is to divide up their A4 sheets of paper into boxes which contain the main areas of design and text.

Revise work on the grammar of slogans and packaging. Ask the children to read out the slogans they have devised and encourage the rest of the class to evaluate them, such as Does it sound right? Then analyse it: What is the subject of the slogan? Is it written, or has it been missed out? Has the verb been left out?

Whole-class skills work

Pick out some of the words that describe the cereals (*healthy, delicious* and so on) and list them on the board or flip chart. Ask the children to think up alternative words or phrases and list them next to the original word. Model the use of a thesaurus to find synonyms. Read out the original phrase, substituting the new word. Has it had any effect on the original meaning? Does the new word work in the context? What happens if the word is left out altogether? Does the phrase make any sense?

Differentiated group activities

1–4*: All the children make any necessary revisions to their plans or text, then draw their cereal packet on an A4 sheet. Children in Group 1 could use photocopiable page 136 (Typefaces) to stimulate further ideas for presenting the text. Children in Group 4 could be helped by giving them a simple template in which the main design areas have been set out in blocks, for example a box at the top for a '10% EXTRA' section, a box for the picture, and an angled box for the brand name.

Conclusion

The children display their cereal packet designs. The class discusses which they would like to buy and why. Which information do they find most useful? Which slogans do they find most persuasive? Why?

TYPEFACES

abcdefghijklmnopqrstuvwxyz
ABCDEFGHIJKLMNOPQRSTUVWXYZ

abcdefghijklmnopqrstuvwxyz
ABCDEFGHIJKLMNOPQRSTUVWXYZ

abcdefghijklmnopqrstuvwxyz
ABCDEFGHIJKLMNOPQRSTUVWXYZ

abcdefghijklmnopqrstuvwxyz
ABCDEFGHIJKLMNOPQRSTUVWXYZ

abcdefghijklmnopqrstuvwxyz
ABCDEFGHIJKLMNOPQRSTUVWXYZ

abcdefghijklmnopqrstuvwxyz
ABCDEFGHIJKLMNOPQRSTUVWXYZ

MAKING NOTES

OBJECTIVES

UNIT	SPELLING/VOCABULARY	GRAMMAR/PUNCTUATION	COMPREHENSION/ COMPOSITION
REFERENCE AND RESEARCH SKILLS Making notes.	Understand the terms 'main idea' and 'key word'.	Identify key words and phrases which are essential to meaning.	Understand the purpose of note-making. Practise note-making.

ORGANIZATION (1 HOUR)

INTRODUCTION	WHOLE-CLASS SKILLS WORK	DIFFERENTIATED GROUP ACTIVITIES	CONCLUSION
Read a message, then delete irrelevant words to reduce it to essential note-form. Discuss the purpose of note-making.	Highlight the main ideas and key words in a non-fiction text. Transfer the information to the Note-taking: Web Chart on photocopiable page 139.	1: Practise note-making using a text of their choice and the web chart. 2 & 3*: As above, with teacher support. 4*: Practise note-making using text selected by the teacher and the adapted web chart.	Review note-making technique. Selected children report on information using their web-chart notes as prompts.

RESOURCES

A page of information text taken from a book on a topic that the children are currently studying, a selection of other information books (at a variety of reading levels) on a current topic, photocopiable page 139 (Note-taking: Web Chart), chalkboard or flip chart, OHP and acetate sheets (optional), writing materials.

PREPARATION

Prepare an OHT (or enlarged A3 photocopy) of a page of information text relevant to a topic the class is currently studying. Write the following message up on the board or flip chart:

> Dear Tom
> Sam telephoned at 6 o'clock. He said that he will meet you outside the new cinema at 8 o'clock. You will find the cinema if you turn left at South Street and then turn right onto Bridge Street. He said that you should remember to bring your wallet!
> > From
> > > Mum

Make enough copies of photocopiable page 139 (Note-taking: Web Chart) for one between two children in Groups 1–3. Adapt the sheet for Group 4 so that they have only one main idea with lines or 'spokes', enlarged to take up the whole page. Choose a suitable piece of text for Group 4 to use in the group session.

Introduction

Show the children the message written on the board or flip chart. Now suggest that Mum has to go out in a hurry and doesn't have time to write the message out in full. What is the essential information she needs to give Tom?

Rub out or delete irrelevant words as the children suggest them, ending up with something like:

> *Tom*
> *Sam phoned 6 o'clock. Will meet you outside*
> *cinema 8 o'clock. Left at South Street, right*
> *onto Bridge Street. Bring wallet!*
> *Mum*

Establish that all the essential information is there, but in shortened note form. The key words and main ideas have been left.

Discuss when else it may be useful to make good notes. Establish that when the children are researching information in books to present later, making notes will help them to retain and remember information more clearly, especially if they organize their note-taking, using a grid or chart.

Whole-class skills work

Display the OHT (or A3 enlargement) of the page of information text you have chosen. Tell the children that they should use the same method as above for picking out the main ideas and key words. What is the main idea of the first paragraph or the key question it answers? (This is usually in the first sentence, but not always!) Underline the key phrases. Then ask what are the key words in the rest of the paragraph that give support or detail to the main idea? Circle those. Continue in a similar manner with the rest of the piece. Next, draw a blank web (like the one on photocopiable page 139) on the board or flip chart. Select children to come up and fill in the web with the information you have highlighted in the text, putting the main ideas in the boxes indicated and writing, in note form, the supporting detail at the end of the spokes.

Differentiated group activities

Children should work in pairs within their ability groups. Give each pair a copy of photocopiable page 139 (Note-taking: Web Chart).
1: Choose an information book from the collection. Use the index to find a sub-topic for investigating. Use the note-taking web to take notes.
2 & 3*: As above, but with teacher support.
4*: Use a suitable text chosen by the teacher to complete the adapted version of the photocopiable page (see 'Preparation').

Conclusion

Discuss how effective it was to use the note-taking method. Resolve any apparent problems. Select children to report information about their topic, using their note-making webs as prompts.

NOTE-MAKING: WEB CHART

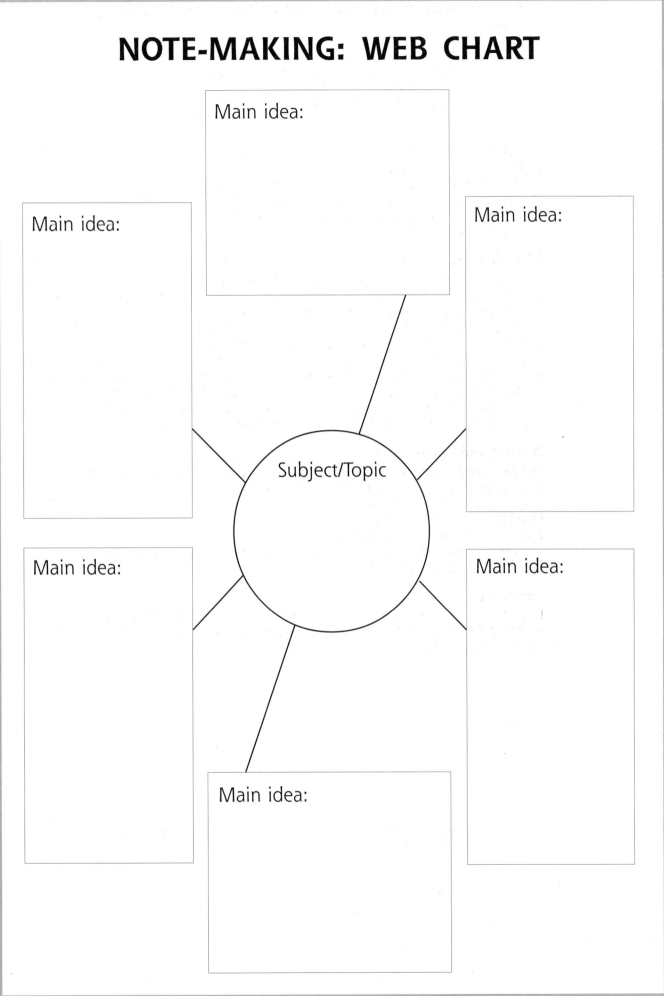

Main idea:

Main idea:

Main idea:

Subject/Topic

Main idea:

Main idea:

Main idea:

REWRITING NURSERY RHYMES

OBJECTIVES

UNIT	SPELLING/VOCABULARY	GRAMMAR/PUNCTUATION	COMPREHENSION/COMPOSITION
WORD PLAY Rewriting nursery rhymes.	Identify rhyme families and note that the same sounds can be spelled in different ways.	Investigate punctuation and determine appropriate punctuation for own poem.	Understand that nursery rhymes are part of the oral tradition. Investigate rhyme patterns and rhymes in nursery rhymes.

ORGANIZATION (1 HOUR)

	INTRODUCTION	WHOLE-CLASS SKILLS WORK	DIFFERENTIATED GROUP ACTIVITIES	CONCLUSION
HOUR 1	Read one of the rewritten nursery rhymes from photocopiable page 142. Brainstorm nursery rhymes from memory. Establish nursery rhymes as part of the oral tradition.	Explore rhythm, rhyme pattern, rhyming words and punctuation in a nursery rhyme. Read the rewritten version on the photocopiable sheet and compare.	1–4*: All pupils rewrite a nursery rhyme of their choice, with the task differentiated according to ability.	Share and evaluate own writing. Decide as a class how to 'publish' the pupil's own nursery rhymes.

RESOURCES

A Big Book of nursery rhymes, photocopiable page 142 (Rewritten Nursery Rhymes), rhyming dictionaries (optional), A3 paper for each child, OHP and acetate (optional), writing materials.

PREPARATION

If possible, prepare an OHT of photocopiable page 142, or enlarge it to A3 size.

Introduction

Display a big book version of a familiar nursery rhyme. Read it through and then ask the children what it is. Establish that it is a nursery rhyme and that they probably learned many of them as small children. How many do they remember well enough to say right through now? Try several. Why do they think they remember them so well? Establish that it is the rhyme and rhythm that make them so memorable. Explain that nursery rhymes are actually little stories made up long, long ago and passed on orally. Regular patterns of rhyme and rhythm made them easier to remember.

Whole-class skills work

Look at the rhymes and rhyme pattern in the nursery rhyme you have displayed. For example:

Mary had a little lamb,
Its fleece was white as snow,
And everywhere that Mary went
The lamb was sure to go.
It followed her to school one day
Which was against the rule.
It made the children laugh and play
To see a lamb at school.

The rhyming words are 'snow' and 'go'; and 'rule' and 'school'. Note that the words rhyme although the spelling of the rhyming sound is different in both cases. Establish that the rhyme pattern is **a b c b**. Ask the children to clap the rhyme as they say it.

Now display photocopiable page 142 with the rewritten version of 'Mary had a little lamb'. Read it through, then ask the children to join in the fun. Explain that the poet here has written a modern version of the traditional rhyme but has kept the rhythm and rhyme pattern as well as the families of rhyming words. Note that the poet has kept the *rule/school* sound, but used *pool/cool* – yet another way of spelling that sound! Draw the children's attention also to the fact that the punctuation of the rewritten version has changed from the original, in order to make the meaning of the 'new story' clearer. Read the other rewritten rhymes on the sheet.

Differentiated group work

1–4: All groups should rewrite a nursery rhyme. First, they should think of a nursery rhyme they know (or find one in a book). They should then write it down (either from memory or copying from a book) on one half of a folded A3 sheet. Then they should think of a way to rewrite it, keeping the rhythm and rhyme pattern, but it is not necessary to keep to the same rhyme families. They may even want to add an extra verse.

The children's rewritten versions should be written on the other half of the A3 sheet. Tell them to look carefully at how they punctuate their poem so that it reads the way they want it to. The children can work individually, in pairs or in small groups, depending on their ability – and, if rhyming dictionaries are available, show the children how to use them.

*The teacher provides support to different groups as necessary.

Conclusion

Ask selected children to recite their original and reworked rhymes. Discuss how well they followed the pattern of their original. Decide as a class how the poems should be kept – as a wall display, perhaps, or bound into a book? Whatever the class decision, allow time for 'publication' outside the hour.

REWRITING NURSERY RHYMES

Mary had a little lamb

Mary had a little lamb,
Its fleece was white as snow,
But Mary had a wild idea.
She'd dye the wool day-glo!
She got a pack of lime green dye
And mixed it in a pool.
It made the children laugh and play
To see a lamb so cool!

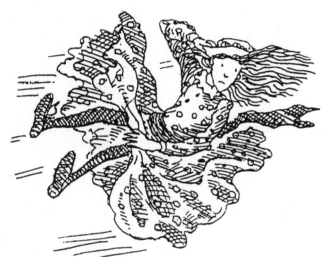

Little Miss Muffet

Little Miss Muffet
Sat on her tuffet
She was fed up with curds and whey
She got thinner and thinner
Without any dinner
And a sudden gust blew her away.

Hey diddle diddle

Hey diddle diddle
The cat lost his fiddle
And started to play on the flute
The little dog wailed
And away he sailed
With the dish and the spoon to Beirut!

I'M ONLY SLEEPING

OBJECTIVES

UNIT	SPELLING/ VOCABULARY	GRAMMAR/ PUNCTUATION	COMPREHENSION/ COMPOSITION
READING POETRY 'I'm Only Sleeping' by John Lennon and Paul McCartney.	Spell words with -ed, -ing, -able suffixes.	Identify nouns and verbs.	Respond to poem by comparing with own experiences. Revise rhyme and couplets.

ORGANIZATION (1 HOUR)

	INTRODUCTION	WHOLE-CLASS SKILLS WORK	DIFFERENTIATED GROUP ACTIVITIES	CONCLUSION
HOUR 1	Shared reading of the poem.	Revise the terms 'rhyme' and 'couplet'. Learn rule for spelling words with -ed, -ing, -able suffixes. Find examples of these words in the poem.	1–4*: Find the couplets in the poem. Find words to do with sleeping and sleepiness. Discuss how pupils feel in the morning.	Discuss how well Lennon and McCartney describe the feeling of sleepiness. Talk about what else the poets are famous for.

RESOURCES

Photocopiable page 146 ('I'm Only Sleeping'), board or flip chart, OHP and acetate (optional), writing materials.

PREPARATION

Prepare enough copies of the poem 'I'm Only Sleeping' (page 146) for one between two children. If possible, prepare the poem as an OHT. Alternatively, enlarge it to A3 size.

Introduction

Display the poem as an OHT or A3 enlargement and share it with the class. Re-read the poem, with the children following line by line. Ask them what they think the poem is about. Establish that it is a poem which describes personal feelings. Explain that it is written in the first-person ('*I'm* only sleeping'; 'When *I* wake up') and describes the poets' feelings when waking up early in the morning. What are those feelings? How do the children feel when they first wake up in the morning? Do they have a similar feeling of drifting in and out of sleep? Do they think the poets have described the feeling well? What do they like about the poem?

Whole-class skills work

Revise the term 'rhyme' (when words end with the same sound we say they rhyme). Ask the children to find examples of rhyming words in the poem. Revise the term 'couplet' (two lines of poetry together which rhyme). Ask the class to find some examples of couplets in the poem.

Point out that there are a lot of words in the poem that end in -*ing*. Some of these are nouns ('morning', 'ceiling', 'feeling') and some are verbs ('yawning', 'sleeping', 'running', 'taking', 'staring', 'staying'). Ask the children to give you the -*ing* words, saying which are nouns and which are verbs. Write them on the board or flip chart under the headings 'Noun' and 'Verb'. Look at the verbs and explain that -*ing* is a suffix that is added to the root verb ('yawn', 'sleep', 'run', 'take', 'stare', 'stay'). Then look particularly at 'take' and 'stare'. Teach the rule: 'When you add a suffix beginning with a vowel (like -ing, -ed, and -able) to a word that ends in a silent e, you drop the e. For example: 'stare/staring', 'take/taking', 'blaze/blazed/blazing', 'love/loved/lovable'.

Differentiated group activities

1–4*: Hand out the photocopies of the poem (one between two children). Then assign some or all of the following activities to each of the groups depending on their ability. Give support where needed.

■ Re-read the poem. Experiment with reading it in 'sleepy' voices.
■ Find and mark all the couplets in the poem.
■ Find lines which are repeated.
■ Find and underline all the words to do with sleeping and sleepiness.
■ Discuss: How do you feel when you wake up in the morning? What do you dream about? Ask more able children more challenging questions such as: How do the poets create the effect of sleepiness? Why are some of the lines repeated? What effect does this have?

Conclusion

Discuss which words and phrases create the feeling of sleepiness and talk about the effect of the repeated lines in the poem. Ask the children if the pattern of the poem reminds them of anything else. Suggest that it is like a song, with a repeated chorus or refrain. (Repetition and parallel structure are features of both music and poetry.) Draw the children's attention to the poets' names. Do the children recognize them? For what are the poets most famous?

FURTHER IDEA

The children could write their own poem about waking up. Some may benefit from using a framework. Tell them to use the first and last line of the Lennon/McCartney poem, but write their own thoughts and feelings in between. Encourage them to concentrate on expressing ideas and emphasize that they should not worry about using rhyme.

I'M ONLY SLEEPING

When I wake up early in the morning,
Lift my head, I'm still yawning.
When I'm in the middle of a dream,
Stay in bed, float up stream,
Please don't wake me, no, don't shake me,
Leave me where I am, I'm only sleeping.
Everybody seems to think I'm lazy.
I don't mind, I think they're crazy
Running everywhere at such a speed,
Till they find there's no need,
Please don't spoil my day, I'm miles away,
And after all, I'm only sleeping.
Keeping an eye on the world going by my window,
Taking my time, lying there and staring at the ceiling,
Waiting for a sleepy feeling.
Please don't spoil my day, I'm miles away,
And after all, I'm only sleeping.
Keeping an eye on the world going by my window,
Taking my time.
When I wake up early in the morning,
Lift my head, I'm still yawning.
When I'm in the middle of a dream,
Staying in bed, float up stream,
Please don't wake me, no, don't shake me,
Leave me where I am, I'm only sleeping.

John Lennon and Paul McCartney

CLERIHEWS

OBJECTIVES

UNIT	SPELLING/VOCABULARY	GRAMMAR/PUNCTUATION	COMPREHENSION/ COMPOSITION
WRITING POETRY Clerihews.	Investigate phonics through rhyme.	Revise using capital letters for new lines of poetry.	Use rhyme effectively in the simplest rhyming form: the clerihew.

ORGANIZATION (1 HOUR)

	INTRODUCTION	WHOLE-CLASS SKILLS WORK	DIFFERENTIATED GROUP ACTIVITIES	CONCLUSION
HOUR 1	Explain what a clerihew is and read the examples to the class.	Revise the terms 'rhyme' and 'couplet'. Investigate phonics through rhyme.	1–4*: All pupils write their own clerihew.	Aim for each pupil to read out one clerihew.

RESOURCES

Photocopiable page 149 (Clerihews), rhyming dictionary (optional), board or flip chart, OHP and acetate (optional), writing materials.

PREPARATION

If possible, make an OHT of the photocopiable page 149 (Clerihews), or enlarge to A3 size.

Introduction

Display the examples of clerihews as an OHT or as an A3 poster and give the following explanation:

Clerihews are funny four-line poems and are named after their inventor, Edmund Clerihew Bentley. They are usually about a famous person, whose name ends the first line.

Edward the Confessor
Slept under the dresser.
When that began to pall,
He slept in the hall.

Edmund Clerihew Bentley

The second line has to rhyme with the first (making the first couplet in the poem). Much of the humour of the clerihew arises from the need to find a rhyme for a person's name, which can be quite difficult (that is why there are very few clerihews about William the Conqueror!).

The clerihew is rounded off by another couplet. The lines can be of any length (though they are usually fairly short), so there is no need to worry about rhythm or the number of syllables.

The clerihews about history and the art of biography show that it is not essential to have a name as a subject. Used in this way, a clerihew is just a short, humorous poem.

Whole-class skills work

Briefly revise the terms 'rhyme' and 'couplet' (see page 144 – 'I'm Only Sleeping' unit), then explore phonics through rhyme. Write a word on the board, for example 'great'. Then ask the children to brainstorm all the rhymes for this that they can think of. This should generate words such as 'late' and 'weight' which show alternative ways of spelling the same ending sound. If you have a rhyming dictionary available, show the children how it works and encourage them to use it to find unusual rhymes.

Differentiated group activities

1–4*: All the children try writing their own clerihews. More able children should have the ability to understand the form from reading the examples on the photocopiable sheet. Less able children can be taken step-by-step through the process in the following way:

- Jot down several names – pop stars, politicians, cartoon characters, historical figures.
- Look them over and see which one suggests a rhyme with amusing possibilities.
- Then develop the idea in lines three and four further.

   If you cannot find a rhyme, try turning the name round, as in the rhyme about Samuel Taylor Coleridge.

   Suggest that the children try writing clerihews on a range of different subjects as well as those about people. Encourage them to use a rhyming dictionary.

Conclusion

Encourage every child to read out one clerihew.

FURTHER IDEA

Suggest to the children that they write a collection of clerihews: 'My family in clerihews' or 'My friends in clerihews'. Finish by binding them into a book.

CLERIHEWS

Sir Francis Drake
Learned to sail on a lake—
But defeating the Armada
Was much harder!
Nicholas Appleby

Edward the Confessor
Slept under the dresser.
When that began to pall,
He slept in the hall.
Edmund Clerihew Bentley

The Art of Biography
Is different from Geography.
Geography is about Maps,
Biography is about Chaps.
Edmund Clerihew Bentley

King Canute
Got a new suit
But it was spoiled because he
Tried to turn back the sea.
Mark Kerridge

Coleridge, Samuel Taylor,
Wrote about an old sailor.
As a Coleridge fan,
I prefer 'Kubla Khan'.
Charles Connell

Bugs Bunny
Thought it was funny
To play in the snow,
But his paws didn't think so!
Matthew Gort

Queen Elizabeth the First
Had a great thirst
So she rushed to the pub
And ordered a pint and some grub.
Mandy Fowler

History
Is a mystery.
Everyone thinks it's boring
And ends up snoring.
Nicholas Key

A NECKLACE OF RAINDROPS

OBJECTIVES

UNIT	SPELLING/VOCABULARY	GRAMMAR/PUNCTUATION	COMPREHENSION/COMPOSITION
READING FICTION AND POETRY Short stories: *A Necklace of Raindrops* by Joan Aiken.	Investigate *-igh*, *-ie* and *-y* rhyming words. Develop vocabulary from reading.	Introduce the term 'simile'. Explore adjectives for colour. Compare adjectives.	Identify themes. Discuss and map out plots. Distinguish fact *versus* fiction. Appreciate the figurative use of language. Compare and contrast stories.

ORGANIZATION (5 HOURS)

	INTRODUCTION	WHOLE-CLASS SKILLS WORK	DIFFERENTIATED GROUP ACTIVITIES	CONCLUSION
HOUR 1	Read 'A Necklace of Raindrops' on pages 13–27. Discuss could it really have happened? Identify realistic and fantasy elements.	Introduce the term 'simile' using examples from the story to build on.	1*: Do a guided re-read of the story and discuss language and ideas. 2 & 3: Write a short sequel to the story. 4*: Do a ten-minute guided re-read of short sections of the story.	One or two pupils from Groups 2 & 3 read out their sequels.
HOUR 2	Read 'The Patchwork Quilt' on pages 106–119.	Compare adjectives using pages 106–107 as a starting point.	1: Write a description of the patchwork quilt. 2 & 3*: Do a guided re-read of the story and discuss it. 4: Cloze exercise.	One or two pupils from Group 1 read out their descriptions of the patchwork quilt.
HOUR 3	Read 'The Cat Sat on the Mat' on pages 28–44.	Work on adjectives for colour using the description of Emma's painting on page 40 as a cloze exercise.	1*: Do a guided re-read of the story and discuss it. 2 & 3: Write what would happen if someone had made a different wish. 4*: Do a guided re-read of the story.	One or two pupils from Groups 2 & 3 read out their versions of the ending of the story based on different wishes being made.
HOUR 4	Read 'There's some Sky in this Pie' on pages 45–55. Look at the cumulative structure of the story and show how it is reflected in the rhyme. What other cumulative fairy stories or nursery rhymes do the pupils know?	Investigate different spellings for *i* sound as in 'ride' (*-igh*, *-ie*, *-y*, *-ye*).	1: Write some extra episodes for the story. 2 & 3*: Do a guided re-read of the story and discuss the language and structure. 4: Make a list of all the creatures who were helped in the story. Invent an extra episode orally, adding to the rhyme.	One or two pupils from Group 1 read out, or tell, their extra episodes.
HOUR 5	Read the blurb on page 5 of the book.	Brainstorm the elements of a book review and devise a template for writing one.	1: Write a free-format book review. 2: Write a book review using a template. 3 & 4*: As for Group 2, but as guided writing.	Selected pupils read out their books reviews. Hold a class vote.

RESOURCES

Photocopiable pages 154 (cloze activity for 'The Patchwork Quilt') and 155 (cloze activity for 'The Cat Sat on the Mat'), enough copies of *A Necklace of Raindrops* by Joan Aiken & Jan Pienkowski (Puffin, ISBN 0-14-030754-0) for half the class, thesauruses, board or flip chart, OHP and acetate (optional), writing materials.

PREPARATION

Make enough copies of 'The Patchwork Quilt' cloze exercise (page 154) for the children in Group 4. Either copy the cloze activity for 'The Cat Sat on the Mat' (page 155) onto acetate or enlarge to A3 size. If you wish the children to complete this activity in pairs, make enough copies for half the class.

Introduction

Read the short story 'A Necklace of Raindrops' on page 13 to the class. This should take about 15 minutes. Encourage the children to listen carefully.

Discuss briefly what sort of story this is: Could it have really happened? Could *parts* of it have happened? Recap on the 'journey' of the necklace: *North Wind, Laura, Meg, Meg's father, silversmith, trader, King of Arabia, Princess of Arabia, Laura.*

Whole-class skills work

Re-read the paragraph at the bottom of page 13, which contains the simile 'hands as cold as ice', and the paragraph at the bottom of page 16, which contains the simile 'she floated like a feather'.

Write the word 'simile' on the board and explain that a simile is a comparison between two things which are unlike in most respects, but have one thing in common. Tell the children that all similes are introduced by the words 'like' or 'as', and are used to make descriptions more vivid – to create pictures in the reader's mind. Discuss what two things are being compared in each of the similes above, identifying what is similar about them.

Brainstorm more similes with the class and write them on the board or flip chart. In each case, discuss what two things are being compared and what is similar about them – their size, their colour, their texture, their smell and so on. You could start with some well-known ones, for example 'as white as snow', 'as quiet as a mouse', 'as sweet as honey'.

Differentiated group activities

1*: Re-read the story with the teacher and answer the following questions as part of a discussion:
■ Why did the North Wind want to do something for Mr Jones?
■ Can you remember what each raindrop enabled Laura to do?
■ Why did Meg steal the necklace? What happened to her?
■ Why did Laura get so much help from the animals?
■ Is there a moral to the story? If so, what do you think it is?
2 & 3: Write a short sequel to the story saying what would happen if Laura received an eleventh raindrop (and a twelfth, if time allows!).
4*: Spend the first ten minutes of the session helping the children to each re-read a short section of the story. At the end of this session, the children carry on reading to the end of the story. Less able readers, can re-read the section you have just read with them.

Conclusion

This will need to be brief to balance the time spent on reading during the introduction and the whole-class skills work. A selected child (or children) from Groups 2 and 3 reads out his/her sequel.

HOUR 2

Introduction
Read 'The Patchwork Quilt' on page 106 with the class. This should take about ten minutes. Encourage the children to listen carefully.

Whole-class skills work
Read the paragraph beginning 'She was making a quilt ...' at the bottom of page 106. Then write the words 'warm', 'warmer', 'warmest' on the board or flip chart. Explain that these words are all adjectives made from the word 'warm'. 'Warm' is an ordinary adjective. 'Warmer' is a comparative adjective that is used when comparing two things. 'Warmest' is a superlative adjective and is used when referring to at least three people or things. The comparative adjective is made by adding -er to the adjective, and the superlative is made by adding -est to the adjective (and putting 'the' in front). Then write 'bright', 'brighter', 'brightest' underneath, followed by 'big', 'bigger', 'biggest'. Ask the children to brainstorm other adjectives that fit this pattern, for example *tall, high, old, long, green, sharp* and so on.

Differentiated group activities
1: Encourage the children to write their own descriptions of a patchwork quilt using some of the descriptive skills studied so far, such as similes and comparative adjectives. If time allows, the children could plan a story around their patchwork quilt descriptions.
2 & 3*: Re-read the story with the teacher and then discuss the language and ideas. Begin by looking at any difficult words and spellings, for example 'sewed' is pronounced differently to the spelling. Look at the movement verbs on pages 116–117, and note how rhyme is used to add to their effect. Look also at the rhyming verses. Then discuss:
■ What kind of a person was Ali Beg?
■ How did he treat his camels?
■ What did the camels decide to do in revenge?
■ Did Ali Beg deserve to get thrown in the sea?
■ How do you think Nils would treat the camels?
4: Each child will need a copy of 'The Patchwork Quilt' cloze exercise on photocopiable page 154. They fill in the gaps with adjectives of their own choice. (They can check later how their versions compare with Joan Aiken's!)

Conclusion
Again, the conclusion needs to be kept brief, so limit it to the reading out of one or two descriptions of the patchwork quilt by the children in Group 1.

HOUR 3

Introduction
Read 'The Cat Sat on the Mat' on page 28 with the class. This should take about 15 minutes. Emphasise that the children must listen carefully.

Whole-class skills work
Begin the session by brainstorming as many colour adjectives as possible. Then display the cloze activity on photocopiable page 155 (The Cat Sat on the Mat). Ask the children to fill in the blanks with their own choices. Encourage them to use the most interesting and imaginative adjectives that they can think of.

Now ask the children to look in thesauruses to see if they can find any other colour words. List these words on the board. Repeat the cloze activity using some different words found in the thesauruses.

Differentiated group activities
1:* Re-read the story independently, then discuss the following questions:
■ How did Emma come to meet the fairy?
■ What gifts did the fairy give to Emma, and what did they do?
■ What kind of a person was Sir Laxton Superb?
■ How did Emma, Aunt Lou and Sam end up living in the sky?
■ What else could they have wished for?
■ What would you have wished for?
2 & 3: Write an alternative ending to the story based on what would have happened if Emma, her aunt, or Sir Laxton Superb had made a different wish.
4*: Re-read the story with the teacher, each child taking a paragraph in turn.

Conclusion

Ask one or two children from Groups 2 and 3 to read out their versions of the ending of the story based on different wishes.

Introduction

Read 'There's some Sky in this Pie' on page 45 with the class, encouraging the children to listen attentively. This should take about ten minutes. Point out how the structure of the story is cumulative, with a new creature being saved by the pie (and added to the rhyme) in each section. Brainstorm other stories and which have a similar structure.

Whole-class skills work

Use the rhyme in the story to investigate the different ways of spelling the long *i* sound as in 'ride'. Write the rhyme on the board or flip chart. Ask the children to read it through with you. Then ask them to identify the rhyming words and underline them: *high, pie, sky, why*. Write *-igh*, *-ie* and *-y* as headings on the board and write 'high', 'pie', 'sky' and 'why' under the appropriate headings. Brainstorm other rhyming words and ask the children to put them under the correct heading. Can they think of any other way of spelling the *i* sound? (For example, -ye as in 'eye' and 'goodbye'.)

Differentiated group activities

1: Think of some other characters who might have been saved by joining the flying pie. Write some extra episodes for the story.

2 & 3*: Re-read the story with the teacher and discuss the following questions:
- Why does the pie fly?
- What other creatures could be included in the story?
- Did you find the ending satisfactory?
- Did you enjoy the story, or did you find it too far-fetched?

4: List all the creatures in the story who were helped. Invent an extra episode orally which involves a new character, then write the rhyme to include this added character.

Conclusion

Selected children from Groups 1 and 4 could read or tell their extra episodes.

Introduction

Now that the class has studied four stories from *A Necklace of Raindrops*, it is a good time to review the book. Read the quotes on the back cover and the text on page 5.

Whole-class skills work

Discuss what the elements of a book review should be. Write them on the board as the children identify them, then order them into a template for writing, for example:
- What is the title?
- Who is the author? Who is the illustrator?
- What kind (genre) of book is it?
- What happens? (Brief outline of plot.)
- What I liked/disliked about the story/illustrations.
- Who I would recommend it to.

Differentiated group activities

1: Write their reviews freely, using the template as a starting point only.
2: Write their reviews following the template closely.
3 & 4*: Follow the template closely in writing reviews, supported by the teacher.

Conclusion

Select some children to read out their book reviews. Hold a class vote on whether the book gets the thumbs up or the thumbs down!

FOLLOW-UP (5 HOURS)

See page 208 which provides a grid plan for a five-hour follow-up unit on the other four stories in *A Necklace of Raindrops*.

THE PATCHWORK QUILT

Far in the north, where the snow falls for three hundred days each year, and all the trees are _____ trees, there was an _____ lady making patchwork. Her name was Mrs Noot. She had many, many little _____ pieces of cloth – boxes full and baskets full, bags full and bundles full, all the colours of the rainbow. There were _____ pieces and _____ pieces, _____ pieces and _____ pieces. Some had flowers on, some were _____.

Mrs Noot sewed twelve pieces into a star. Then she sewed the stars together to make _____ stars. And then she sewed *those* together. She sewed them with _____ thread and _____ thread and _____ thread and _____ thread.

What do you suppose she was making?

She was making a quilt for the bed of her _____ grandson Nils. She had nearly finished. When she had put in the last star, little Nils would have the biggest and _____ and warmest and most _____ quilt in the whole of the north country – perhaps in the whole world.

(from pages 106–107 of 'The Patchwork Quilt' from the Puffin Book edition of *A Necklace of Raindrops* by Joan Aiken © Joan Aiken, 1968, published by Puffin Books, 1975)

THE CAT SAT ON THE MAT

There was once a little girl called Emma Pippin. She had

_____ rosy cheeks and _____ hair and

she lived with her Aunt Lou. They were very poor, too

poor to buy a house, so they lived in an old bus. The

engine would not go, but it was a nice old bus and they

loved it. The outside of the bus was painted

_____, the inside was painted _____, and

the windows had _____ curtains. There was a

stove, which kept them warm, and the smoke went out of

a chimney in the roof.

   The bus stood by a high, _____ wall. Inside

this wall were many lovely _____ apple trees, on

which were growing many lovely _____ apples.

(from pages 28–29 of 'The Cat Sat on the Mat' from the Puffin Book edition of *A Necklace of Raindrops* by Joan Aiken, © Joan Aiken, 1968, published by Puffin Books 1975)

PROVERBS

OBJECTIVES

UNIT	SPELLING/VOCABULARY	GRAMMAR/PUNCTUATION	COMPREHENSION/ COMPOSITION
WRITING FICTION Write a story with a defined ending based on a proverb.	Identify misspelled words in own writing. Develop vocabulary from reading.	Understand the figurative use of words. Use the Redrafting Checklist as a basis for revision of key writing skills.	Understand the figurative nature of proverbs. Write stories which end with a proverb.

ORGANIZATION (3 HOURS)

	INTRODUCTION	WHOLE-CLASS SKILLS WORK	DIFFERENTIATED GROUP ACTIVITIES	CONCLUSION
HOUR 1	Read and discuss the list of proverbs.	Revise previous work on story structure.	1–4*: Pupils discuss the proverbs in groups and make up brief stories as examples.	Each group shares one of its stories with the class.
HOUR 2	Display the Story Planner and remind pupils of its use.	Pupils plan their stories using the Story Planner.	1–4: All pupils begin to write their stories. *The teacher supports Groups 1 & 4.	Selected pupils read out the beginnings of their stories and explain how they intend to develop them.
HOUR 3	Display the Redrafting Checklist and explain how to use it.	Use the Redrafting Checklist as a basis for revision of key writing skills.	1–4: All pupils finish/ redraft their stories. *The teacher supports Groups 2 & 3.	Selected pupils read out their completed stories.

RESOURCES

Photocopiable pages 159 (Proverbs), 160 (Redrafting Checklist) and 161 (Story Planner from 'Myth-maker' unit, Term 2), OHP and acetate (optional), writing materials.

PREPARATION

Prepare enough copies of photocopiable page 159 (Proverbs) for one between two children, and, if possible, also prepare it as an OHT. Alternatively, enlarge it to A3 size. Prepare enough copies of the Redrafting Checklist (page 160) and the Story Planner (page 95 from the 'Myth-maker' unit, Term 2) for one per child. Prepare the Story Planner as an OHT or enlarge it to A3 size.

The Redrafting Checklist should also be prepared as an OHT or enlarged to A3 size. However, when photocopied for the children, it should be customized for each group according to their ability.

Children in Group 1 could use the sheet as it stands, but children in Group 4 would be better served by a version with several more demanding items omitted, for example:

- CAPITAL LETTERS: delete bullet point 4.
- PARAGRAPHS: delete bullet point 3.
- PUNCTUATION: delete bullet points 4 and 5.
- APOSTROPHES: delete bullet point 2.
- VOCABULARY: delete bullet point 2.

Introduction

Display the list of proverbs as an OHT or A3 enlargement and begin the session by explaining that a proverb is a short, well-known saying illustrating a popular belief. Say that proverbs provide a store of common wisdom that is passed on from generation to generation by word of mouth.

Do not read through the list one by one, but pick out a couple of proverbs that interest you from the first section and explain what they mean by giving examples. The proverbs in the second section are more difficult to understand as they use language in a figurative way. Explain one or two of these as well. Then ask a few children if they can explain the meaning of two or three more selected proverbs from this section.

Whole-class skills work

Explain that proverbs often make good endings to stories because they can sum up what a story is about. Review previous work on story structure by asking the children what else a story needs. Give out one copy of photocopiable page 159 (Proverbs) per pair, and explain that you want the children to choose a proverb as the ending to a story they are going to write.

Differentiated group activities

1–3*: Work in sub-groups of four to read and discuss the proverbs in the second section of the photocopiable sheet. The teacher supports Groups 1 to 3 and helps the children to follow these instructions:
■ Take it in turns to pick out a proverb and explain what you think it means.
■ Discuss other children's explanations of proverbs. Help them to get the meaning clear. (This may require teacher support.)
■ Go round again, but this time make up a little story to illustrate your proverb.
4*: As above, including teacher support, but use the first section of the list which includes proverbs with a literal meaning. Those children in Group 3 who are having trouble with figurative proverbs should also use only the first section of the sheet.

Conclusion

Each group should present one of its stories orally to the whole class. Follow with a discussion and evaluation based on the question 'Was the story a good example of the proverb?'

Introduction and whole-class skills work

Display the Story Planner from the 'Myth-maker' unit, Term 2 as an OHT or A3 enlargement. Remind the children how to use it. Demonstrate how to develop a plan for a longer, written story using the Story Planner and one of the oral stories presented in the Conclusion of Hour 1. Then ask the children to choose one of their oral stories and develop it in a similar way, using their copy of the Story Planner sheet. Help them to ensure that they build up effective character and place descriptions and that they present a problem to be solved in the middle of their story. Explain that the ending of their story should lead up to a statement of the proverb. Ask the children to write this statement at the end of the final box on their Story Planner sheet.

Differentiated group activities

1–4: All children begin to write their stories. *The teacher supports Groups 1 and 4.

Conclusion

Selected children read out the beginnings of their stories and explain how they intend to develop them.

PROVERBS

Introduction
Display the Redafting Checklist as an OHT or A3 enlargement and explain how to use it (be sure to point out that each group has a version appropriate to its needs – see 'Preparation', above). Explain that the checklist is to be used with a partner to check important aspects of their stories written in Hour 2. To complete part 1, each child should read his/her story to a partner who should then comment on the content. Emphasize that in this lesson, this will be the story structure and how effectively it leads up to the proverb at the end.

To complete part 2, explain that each pair should check the story together against the checklist items. (These items are simply a summary of the key skills covered so far, as there is not space to include every skill.)

Whole-class skills work
Use part 2 of the Redrafting Checklist as a focus for the revision of key writing skills. Give most emphasis to the basic points which are included on all the versions of the checklist.

Differentiated group activities
1–4: All children finish and redraft their stories using the Redrafting Checklist. *The teacher supports Groups 2 and 3.

Conclusion
Selected children read out their completed stories.

PROVERBS

All's well that ends well.
Beggars can't be choosers.
The best things in life are free.
Better safe than sorry.
Early to bed and early to rise makes a man healthy,
    wealthy, and wise.
A friend in need is a friend indeed.
If at first you don't succeed, try, try again.
Look before you leap.
Many hands make light work.
Never put off until tomorrow what you can do today.
One good turn deserves another.
Practice makes perfect.
Two wrongs don't make a right.
There's no place like home.

All that glitters is not gold.
The bigger they come the harder they fall.
Every cloud has a silver lining.
The grass is always greener on the other side of the fence.
Great oaks from little acorns grow.
There's more than one way to skin a cat.
Once bitten, twice shy.
One man's meat is another man's poison.
One rotten apple spoils the barrel.
Rome wasn't built in a day.
You can't fit a round peg in a square hole.
A stitch in time saves nine.
Walls have ears.
Well begun is half done.

REDRAFTING CHECKLIST

PART 1
Read your work to your partner. Ask him or her to say what they thought of your writing and jot down these comments in the box below.

PART 2
Read through your writing with your partner and check the following:

CAPITAL LETTERS   Have you used capital letters for:
- beginning sentences? ☐
- names? ☐
- places? ☐
- days, months, special occasions? ☐

PARAGRAPHS   Have you:
- indented the first line of a paragraph? ☐
- remembered not to leave whole blank lines between paragraphs? ☐
- started a new paragraph for a new topic, or a new scene in a story? ☐

PUNCTUATION   Have you:
- used a full stop at the end of sentences? ☐
- used questions marks at the end of questions? ☐
- used speech marks before and after words actually spoken? ☐
- begun speech with a capital letter? ☐
- placed a comma, full stop, question mark or exclamation mark before final speech marks? ☐

APOSTROPHES   Have you:
- used an apostrophe to show missing letters in contractions? ☐
- used an apostrophe after a name to show ownership? ☐

VOCABULARY   Have you:
- used some interesting adjectives? ☐
- used some synonyms for 'said'? ☐

SPELLING   Have you:
- checked your spelling? ☐

THE SEASHORE

OBJECTIVES

UNIT	SPELLING/VOCABULARY	GRAMMAR/PUNCTUATION	COMPREHENSION/ COMPOSITION
READING NON-FICTION Information genre: *The Seashore* by Jane Walker.	Revise the terms 'heading', 'illustration' and 'caption'. Learn the terms 'sub-heading', 'font' and 'double-page spread'. Glossary Exercise on difficult words and terms in the text.	Use of present tense in information genre.	Reading information genre: understanding and using reference aids, eg contents, index and glossary. Understand how page design is used to present information clearly.

ORGANIZATION (4 HOUR)

	INTRODUCTION	WHOLE-CLASS SKILLS WORK	DIFFERENTIATED GROUP ACTIVITIES	CONCLUSION
HOUR 1	Read 'Inside a Rockpool' (doublepagespread) on photocopiable pages 164–165. Discuss layout.	Revise the following terms: 'heading', 'illustration' and 'caption'. Teach the terms 'sub-heading', 'font', 'double-page spread'. Pupils find examples in the text and suggest reasons for the different font sizes.	1*: Part B of Reading Comprehension sheet. 2: Part C of Reading Comprehension sheet. 3*: Page Design Exercise. 4: Re-read 'Inside a Rockpool' and do part A of Reading Comprehension sheet.	Discuss how the signposting of books with titles, captions and different font sizes helps to make information retrieval easier.
HOUR 2	Examine the contents, index and glossary pages of *The Seashore*. Discuss their uses.	Index and glossary exercise (a minimum of one text per group is needed).	1: Re-read 'Inside a Rockpool' and do part A of Reading Comprehension sheet. 2*: Do part B of Reading Comprehension sheet. 3: Using additional texts, do part C of Reading Comprehension sheet. 4*: Do the Page Design Exercise.	Discuss the information retrieved from the additional texts by Groups 2 & 3.
HOUR 3	Examine the book as a whole: look at cover design, introduction, 'blurb' and a range of page layouts.	Revise the present tense. Examine text for examples of verbs in the present tense.	1*: Page Design Exercise. 2: Re-read 'Inside a Rockpool' and do part A of Reading Comprehension sheet. 3*: Part B of Reading Comprehension sheet. 4: Part C of Reading Comprehension sheet.	Discuss the results of the Page Design Exercise, looking at examples produced by Groups 1, 3 & 4.
HOUR 4	Read an account of a rockpool from one of the additional books.	Compare the information given in *The Seashore* and in the additional book.	1: Part C of Reading Comprehension sheet. 2*: Page Design Exercise. 3: Re-read 'Inside a Rockpool' and do part A of Reading Comprehension sheet. 4*: Using the texts, do part B of Reading Comprehension sheet.	Go over answers to parts A & B of Comprehension

RESOURCES

Photocopiable pages 164–165 ('Inside a Rockpool'), 166 (Reading Comprehension), 167 (Index Exercise) and 168–169 (Page Design Exercise), set of dictionaries, group set of *The Seashore* by Jane Walker (ISBN 0-7496-1450-1) (minimum one between two for the largest group), selection of other reference books about the seashore (including ones with details about rockpools), A3 sheet of paper per pair of children, scissors and paste, writing materials.

PREPARATION

Copy the Reading Comprehension sheet (page 166), allowing one per child. Prepare enough copies of the other photocopiable sheets (pages 164–165, 167 and 168–169) listed above for one between two children.

Introduction

Read 'Inside a Rockpool' (photocopiable pages 164–165) with the children following on their own copies. Note that this text is based on pages 10 and 11 of *The Seashore*.

Whole-class skills work

Revise the terms 'heading', 'illustration' and 'caption', and teach the terms 'subheading' and 'font'. Explain that 'font' means the style of the printed text. (If necessary, show the children some examples of different typefaces used in books to make the idea clearer. Explain to them that the term 'font' is often used instead of typeface – especially in computer terminology.) Tell the children that the main emphasis in this lesson is to look for different sizes of font.

Ask the children to find examples of headings, subheadings, illustrations and captions on their copies of 'Inside a Rockpool' spread, and to suggest reasons for the different font sizes.

Differentiated group activities

1*: Do part B of the Reading Comprehension sheet using the group set of texts.
2: Do part C of the Reading Comprehension sheet using the additional information texts on the theme of the seashore.
3*: Do the Page Design exercise. The children will see that the two photocopiable pages for this activity contain all the elements for a reference book double-page spread. Working in pairs, the children cut them out and assemble them onto a sheet of A3 paper (folded down the middle) to make a clear and attractive page design. Explain that the main text for this exercise is provided in one long column. The children can cut this column into blocks of any size they wish, but must make sure that the text flows on correctly wherever they place it. Point out that captions should be matched to illustrations. Subheadings should be put in the appropriate places or left out altogether, depending on the children's ability.
4: Re-read and discuss 'Inside a Rockpool', then do part A of the Reading Comprehension sheet.

Conclusion

Discuss how the signposting of books with titles, captions and different font sizes helps to make information retrieval easier.

Introduction

Provide a minimum of one copy of *The Seashore* per group and examine the Contents, Index and Glossary pages. Discuss their uses.

Whole-class skills work

Explain to the children how to use an index by going through the bullet points on the Index Exercise on the photocopiable sheet on page 167. Ask the children to then carry out the exercise using one photocopiable sheet between two, sitting in their normal groups so that they can share the copies of *The Seashore* text. The children can take it in turns to look up the information, assisted by the nearest group members. Initially, the children in Group 4 should concentrate on looking up the first four items listed on the sheet.

The children can follow up the activity with the Glossary Exercise on the same sheet, for which dictionaries will be needed. This exercise serves two purposes: it helps children to learn difficult terms and words in the text, and it helps them to grasp the concept of a glossary.

Differentiated group activities

1: Re-read 'Inside a Rockpool' and do part A of the Reading Comprehension sheet.
2*: Do part B of the Reading Comprehension sheet using the group set of texts.
3: Do part C of the Reading Comprehension sheet using the additional texts.
4*: Do the Page Design Exercise (see the activity for Group 3 in 'Hour 1' for details).

Conclusion

Discuss the information retrieved from the additional texts by Groups 2 and 3. Does it add anything to the knowledge they have gained from *The Seashore*?

Introduction

Examine *The Seashore* as a whole: look at the cover design, introduction, 'blurb' and a range of its page layouts.

Whole-class skills work

Revise the present tense. Write the first sentence of page 4 on the board or chart: 'The seashore is the place where the land meets the sea or ocean'. Ask the children which word is the verb and what tense the verb is in. (The main verb is 'is', although the children may pick out 'meets' as well.)

Encourage the children to examine the 'Inside a Rockpool' text on the photocopiable pages for other examples of verbs in the present tense. Point out that, although the past tense is sometimes used, use of the present tense is one of the standard features of information writing.

Differentiated group activities

1*: Do the Page Design Exercise (see 'Hour 1' for details).
2: Re-read 'Inside a Rockpool' and do part A of the Reading Comprehension sheet.
3*: Do part B of the Reading Comprehension sheet using the group set of texts.
4: Do part C of the Reading Comprehension sheet using the additional texts.

Conclusion

Share different page designs from Groups 1, 3 and 4. Point out that information writing makes use of clear explanation in the present tense, and is often helped by page layout, illustrations, and reference aids such as contents, glossaries and indexes.

Introduction

Read to the children an account of a rockpool from one of the other reference books.

Whole-class skills work

In a brief discussion, compare the information given by the above book with that found in *The Seashore*. The key point to bring out is that both give useful information, and that more can be learned from two books than from one. In other words, when researching, try to use a variety of sources.

Differentiated group activities

1: Do part C of the Reading Comprehension sheet using the additional texts.
2*: Do the Page Design exercise (see 'Hour 1' for details).
3: Re-read 'Inside a Rockpool' and do part A of the Reading Comprehension sheet.
4*: Do part B of the Reading Comprehension sheet using the texts.

Conclusion

Now that the whole class has completed the Reading Comprehension sheet, this is the ideal opportunity to go over it with a particular focus on parts A and B.

FURTHER IDEAS

The same process could be applied to a non-fiction text which is being used for the study of another curriculum area.
NB: If you intend to do the next unit 'Words in Windows', you will need to keep the children's work from the Page Design Exercise.

INSIDE A ROCKPOOL

INSIDE A ROCKPOOL

Along a rocky seashore there are dozens of rockpools filled with seawater at low tide. Rockpools are interesting places to explore. Limpets and winkles feed on tiny pieces of seaweed, and in turn provide food for flesh-eating animals such as starfish and whelks. Small fish and crabs hunt shrimps and other tiny creatures hiding among the seaweed.

Rockpool hunters

In deeper pools, hunting fish like sea scorpions and weever fish lie in wait for any small fish that swims past. Dog whelks crawl over the rocks in search of a meal of barnacles or mussels. Sea anemones wait patiently to trap shrimps and small fish in their tentacles.

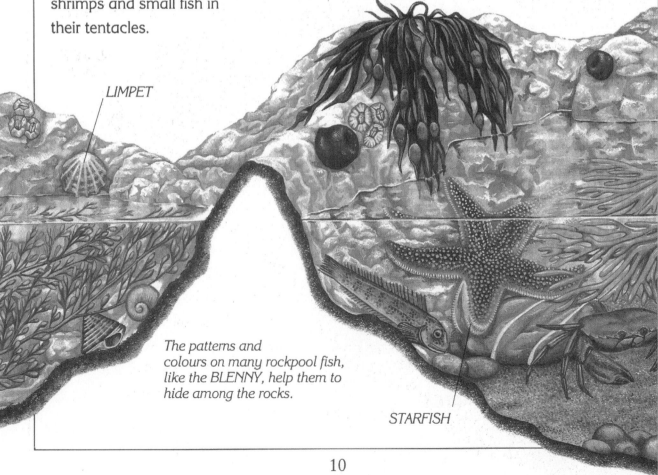

LIMPET

The patterns and colours on many rockpool fish, like the BLENNY, help them to hide among the rocks.

STARFISH

10

INSIDE A ROCKPOOL

A seaweed called PACIFIC GIANT KELP can grow to over 60 metres in length.

A pool survey

Next time you visit the seashore, try making a survey of the life inside a rockpool. Sketch the outline of a rockpool and look closely at each part (and under the seaweed) to find out which creatures and plants live in it. Add these to your rockpool sketch.

BARNACLES

Inside each ROCKPOOL lives a whole community of plants and animals. Many depend on each other for food and shelter.

BLADDER WRACK

A place to hide

Seaweeds like bladder wrack (above) are often found in rockpools. They provide shelter for small shrimps and prawns, which hide from hungry crabs and hunting fish like shannies and rocklings.

PRAWN

SEA ANEMONE

11

READING COMPREHENSION

PART A

Look at the 'Inside a Rockpool' photocopiable pages (or pages 10–11 of *The Seashore* book), and answer these questions:

■ Make a list of all the creatures which hunt for food in rockpools.

■ Find the picture of the sea anemone and describe it in your own words.

■ How do sea anemones catch their food?

■ How do blenny fish hide from other creatures who would like to eat them?

■ Look at the picture of the rockpool and make a list of all the creatures you can see.

PART B

Use the Contents and Index pages of *The Seashore* to help you find the answers to these questions:

■ Make a list of creatures that have shells.

■ Why do many seashore creatures have shells?

■ How are pearls formed?

■ Make a list of birds that are found along the seashore.

■ What is the connection between Samuel Taylor Coleridge and the albatross?

■ Why do different birds have differently shaped bills (beaks)?

■ Who was Robinson Crusoe?

PART C

Look through the other books on the same subject and see what you can find out about:

■ Rockpools.

■ Seashore birds.

■ Seashore fish.

■ Seashore plants.

■ Creatures with shells.

INDEX EXERCISE

Use the INDEX (page 32) and the GLOSSARY (page 31) to write some brief information for all the items listed in column 1. Here are some tips to help you:

■ Look up the word in the index. This will give you one or more page numbers.

■ Find the page, then *scan* the page for the word.

■ Read the paragraph and pick out one or two key facts.

■ Write the facts in column 2.

■ When the index gives you more than one page number, look at all the pages and pick out one or two of the most important facts.

COLUMN 1: ITEM	COLUMN 2: INFORMATION
Butterfish	
Walrus	
Eskimos	
Amundsen	
Sea Stack	

GLOSSARY EXERCISE

■ With a partner, browse through the book and make a list of ten words you don't understand.

■ Look the words up in the Glossary on page 31. If they are not there, look them up in a dictionary.

■ Put them in alphabetical order, then rewrite their meanings and give your list the title 'Glossary'.

PAGE DESIGN EXERCISE

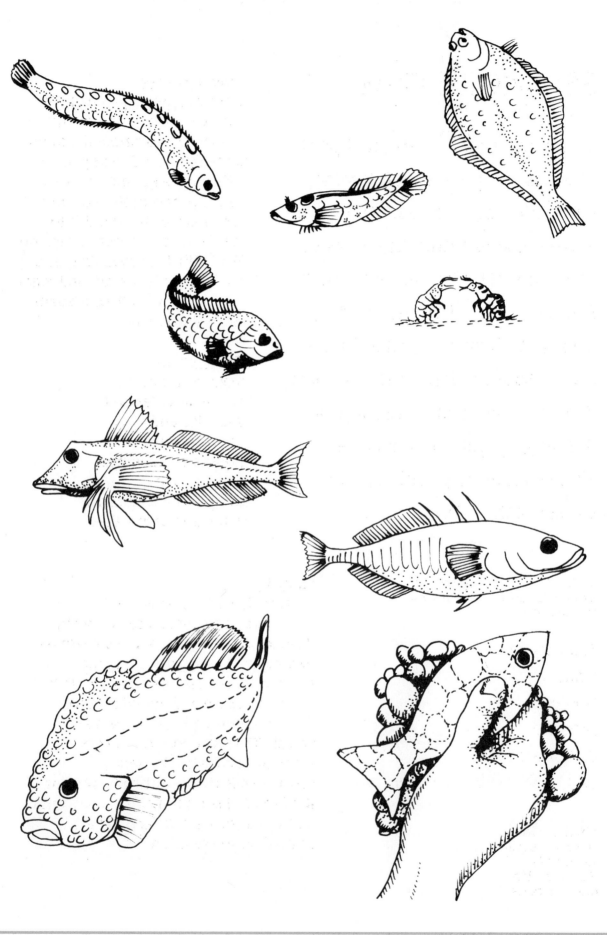

PAGE DESIGN EXERCISE

SEASHORE FISH

Seashore fish live in the rockpools and shallow puddles left behind when the tide goes out. Waves can wash these fish onto the rocks or sand. The clingfish and lumpsucker fish have special disc-shaped suckers to help them cling to the rocks. Another danger facing these fish are hunters looking for food. Scavenging gulls and eels are always ready to gobble up any small seashore fish.

The CHAMELEON SHRIMP changes the size of its coloured spots to match its surroundings.

TUB GUNNARD

WRASSE

LUMPSUCKER

SAND EEL

CLINGFISH

DAB

BUTTERFISH hide under stones and seaweeds in shallow pools on rocky seashores.

Hide and seek
You can make a game of hide and seek with cardboard fish on a coloured background. Cut out some fish shapes and paint a different background on four large squares of stiff paper or card. Now paint your fish to match the backgrounds. Lay the fish on their surroundings and see if your friends can find them. The person who finds the most fish is the winner.

Food for fish
Small fish, such as sticklebacks (above), shannies and rocklings, feed on prawns and shrimps. They hunt in rockpools and shallow water and at low tide.

Flatfish
Larger fish, such as wrasse, tub gunnard and sea-bass, usually live in deeper water out to sea, but sometimes visit the shallow waters along the seashore when the tide comes in. Fish like dabs, plaice and flounders have thin, flat bodies and are known as flatfish. The colourings on the skin of many flatfish match the sandy surroundings of the seabed. This helps the fish to hide from their enemies, but it also makes them difficult to be noticed on the seashore.

WORDS IN WINDOWS

OBJECTIVES

UNIT	SPELLING/VOCABULARY	GRAMMAR/PUNCTUATION	COMPREHENSION/ COMPOSITION
WRITING NON-FICTION Explanation genre: Words in Windows.	Revise the terms 'heading', 'subheading', 'illustration', 'caption', 'font'. Introduce the term 'body text'.		Present information and explanations in the style of modern reference books.

ORGANIZATION (2 HOURS)

	INTRODUCTION	WHOLE-CLASS SKILLS WORK	DIFFERENTIATED GROUP ACTIVITIES	CONCLUSION
HOUR 1	Look again at 'Inside a Rockpool' from pages 10–11 of *The Seashore* (used in the previous unit) or a similar page in a modern children's reference book.	Revise skills: use of contents, index, glossary and note-taking.	1–4: All groups prepare to produce a reference book entitled *Life in the Sea* through researching their allocated topics. *The teacher supports Group 4.	Discuss progress so far and share solutions to any problems encountered. Discuss any new terms or devices pupils may have come across.
HOUR 2	Display a selection of page layouts from the Page Design Exercise in the previous unit 'The Seashore'.	Revise the terms 'heading', 'subheading', 'illustration', 'caption', 'font' etc. Introduce the term 'body text'. Pupils point out examples in each other's page layouts.	1: Design own reference book double-page spread. 2 & 3*: Guided writing of a reference book spread on the Words in Windows template, adapting as necessary. 4: As above, but keep to the format of the template.	Share examples of the reference book pages.

RESOURCES

This unit can be used as an immediate follow-up exercise to the previous unit 'The Seashore', or it can be used on it's own with a different reference text as the focus. If it is used as a follow-up to 'The Seashore', you will need the group set of *The Seashore* and children's work from the Page Design Exercise. Additional reference books on sea creatures will also be needed.

If this unit is being used as a stand alone (that is, in the context of a topic being studied in another area of the curriculum), the exemplar reference book should be on that topic but of a similar modern style to *The Seashore.*

An OHP and acetate would be useful for discussing specific pages with the whole class. Alternatively, make A3 enlargements. You will also need photocopiable page 172 (Words in Windows) and writing materials, including paper for Group 1 who will not be using the template.

PREPARATION

Prepare enough copies of photocopiable page 172 (Words in Windows) for two per child. Prepare as OHTs or A3 enlargements any specific pages from *The Seashore* (or similar reference book) that you wish to discuss in the introduction.

Introduction

Look again at 'Inside a Rockpool' (pages 10–11 in *The Seashore)* or some similar pages in a reference book related to your chosen topic. Look also at the reference aids such as the contents, index and glossary pages.

Whole-class skills work

Explain to the class that each group is going to write a reference book and that the first step is to research the information. Revise with them the following research skills:
- Use the index and contents pages to find out where to look.
- Use the glossary and a dictionary to help with unknown words.
- Do not copy the text; make notes instead. Put the book away. Then write sentences from your notes.
- Another way to avoid copying is to describe a picture in your own words.

Differentiated group activities

1–4: Tell the class that their reference books will be entitled *Life in the Sea* (see 'Further ideas' for suggestions based on a humanities topic). Each child in the group should contribute a page on one of the following sea creatures:
- albatross
- butterfish
- crabs
- arctic tern
- clams
- lobsters and so on.

The first step is to research the topic using the skills taught in the previous session. (Basic information about these skills can be found in *The Seashore*.) Children in Groups 1–3 should be encouraged to look in other reference books and write in more detail.
*The teacher supports children in Group 4.

Conclusion

Discuss progress so far. Are the children encountering any problems in finding and/or noting down their information? Do they share successful solutions? Have they found any stylistic devices not yet discussed?

Introduction

Give out the work from the Page Design Exercise (done in the previous unit), but do this randomly so that each child receives another's work. The children will work in fours and use these as a basis for discussion. An OHT of one or two examples of the children's page layouts would provide a good starting point and a convenient way of introducing the skills work.

Whole-class skills work

Revise the terms 'heading', 'subheading', 'illustration', 'caption', 'font' and 'double-page spread', and introduce the term body text. Ask the children to find examples of these elements in the Page Design Exercises. They should also discuss how clear each page layout is.

Differentiated group activities

1: The children design their own pages for the *Life in the Sea* reference book using ideas from the introduction and skills session. They then write up their notes on the pages they have designed.
2 & 3*: With the support of the teacher, the children write their reference book pages on the photocopiable templates provided. They should feel free to adapt them and should aim to write two pages.
4: The children write on the template exactly as it is and aim to complete one page.

Conclusion

The children share examples of their reference book pages. Allow some extra time for the children to bind their pages together to make a classroom reference book. This activity can either follow on at the end of the session or be carried out at a later time.

FURTHER IDEAS

The skills taught in this unit should be employed soon afterwards in the context of another curriculum topic in which writing plays an important part. Each group could then produce its own reference book for that topic with each child in the group writing a page about a sub-topic. For example, if the topic is a history one on 'Egypt', different children in the group could write pages on the Pharaohs, the Pyramids, mummies, Egyptian costume, Egyptian homes, the Nile and so on.

WORDS IN WINDOWS

Key facts

DICTIONARY WORK

OBJECTIVES

UNIT	SPELLING/VOCABULARY	GRAMMAR/PUNCTUATION	COMPREHENSION/ COMPOSITION
REFERENCE AND RESEARCH SKILLS Dictionary work.	To know and use words and phrases related to dictionary parts: 'guide word', 'headword', 'pronunciation', 'accent', 'syllable', 'definition', 'part of speech', 'origin'.	To understand the layout of a dictionary entry.	To understand that some dictionaries provide further information about words.

ORGANIZATION (1 HOUR)

INTRODUCTION	WHOLE-CLASS SKILLS WORK	DIFFERENTIATED GROUP ACTIVITIES	CONCLUSION
Read and explore a dictionary page to establish its purpose and features.	Label features of dictionary entries.	1–4: All groups work at own level, choosing words from own reading books at random to explore in dictionary. *The teacher works with Groups 1 & 4.	Review of appropriate vocabulary for discussion dictionary entries.

HOUR 1

RESOURCES

Enough dictionaries for at least one between two children (differentiate the levels of these to cater for the range of abilities), current reading book for each child, board or flip chart, OHP and acetate (optional), writing materials.

PREPARATION

Find a page or double-page spread from one of the class dictionaries that has all the features you wish to discuss in the lesson, for example guide words at the top of the page, headword, pronunciation guide, syllabication, part of speech, words with multiple meanings, sentences to exemplify meaning, word origins and so on. Ideally, prepare it as an OHT. Otherwise photocopy it and enlarge as much as possible. In addition, write out one of the entries on the board or flip chart, for example:

pupil pu´-pil (pyoopil) *n.* 1. A person who is learning from a teacher: *The pupil asked the teacher a question.* 2. A hole in the centre of the eyeball through which light enters the eye: *The bright light made his pupils go very small.* [from Latin *pupilla* – little girl or doll]

Introduction

Display the OHT or enlarged copy of the dictionary page or spread. Establish that it is a page from a dictionary. Ask 'What is a dictionary?' Collaborate to come up with a suitable definition, for example 'A dictionary is a book of words in which the words are listed in alphabetical order and their meanings given.' Choose several words on the page displayed and ask the children for definitions. Then ask 'Is that the only information the dictionary gives?' Establish that the dictionary provides quite a lot more information.

Whole-class skills work

Focus this session on establishing how a dictionary page works and developing appropriate vocabulary to talk about it, for example 'guide words', 'entry', 'headwords', 'pronunciation guide' (including 'accent' and 'syllables'), 'part of speech', 'definition' (including 'multiple meanings'), 'sentences to show meaning', 'word origins' and so on. Draw arrows and label all these parts on the example you have written out on the board or flip chart.

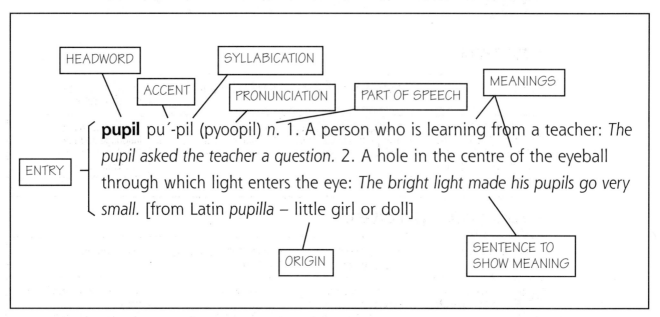

Differentiated group activities

Each group works with a dictionary appropriate for its level of ability.

1*: Each child opens their current reading book at random. They close their eyes and place their finger on the page. Then they write down the word. They choose three words in this manner, then write dictionary entries for them using the model illustrated above. When they have finished, they compare their work with entries for the same words in their own dictionary.

2 & 3: Choose three words as described for Group 1. Look up the words in the dictionary. For each word, write out the whole entry. Say what the guide words on the dictionary page are for each one, and label each part of the entry as in the example above. (The teacher will need to make sure the children understand which features of the above example are included in their dictionaries.)

4*: As for Groups 2 and 3, using simplified dictionaries. Make sure the children understand which features of the above illustrated example are included in their dictionaries.

Conclusion

Using examples of the children's work from the group activities, review the dictionary vocabulary taught in the lesson, ensuring that the children can match the words that describe features of dictionary entries with the features themselves.

ROBIN HOOD

OBJECTIVES

UNIT	SPELLING/VOCABULARY	GRAMMAR/PUNCTUATION	COMPREHENSION/ COMPOSITION
READING FICTION Long-established fiction (Adventure): *Robin Hood and the Sheriff* by Julian Atterton.	Develop vocabulary from text, particularly archaic words and phrases.	Pronouns. Revision of parts of speech: nouns, adjectives, verbs.	Study plot, character, language and ideas. Develop literal and inferential comprehension. Write a book review.

ORGANIZATION (5 HOURS)

	INTRODUCTION	WHOLE-CLASS SKILLS WORK	DIFFERENTIATED GROUP ACTIVITIES	CONCLUSION
HOUR 1	Discuss what pupils already know about Robin Hood. Reconstruct an outline of his story orally. Read 'Robin Hood and the Sheriff', pages 9–30.	Study vocabulary, particularly archaic words and phrases in text.	1*: Complete Characters sheet. 2 & 3: Complete parts A and B of Reading Comprehension sheet. 4*: Complete part A of Reading Comprehension sheet.	Talk about key ideas in the story. Discussion behaviour of Robin Hood: Why did he not rob Sir Richard?
HOUR 2	Recap on the story so far, then read 'Robin Hood and the Sheriff', pages 31–49.	Pronouns, part 1.	1: Complete all parts of Reading Comprehension sheet. 2 & 3*: Complete Characters sheet. 4: Design a 'Wanted' poster for Robin Hood.	Talk about the ideas in the story: Why did Robin Hood rob the Sheriff?
HOUR 3	Read 'The Golden Arrow', pages 53–73.	Identify new vocabulary. Pronouns, part 2.	1*: Write character study of Maid Marion. 2 & 3: Write 'The Nottingham News' front page for the day. 4*: Design advertisement for Nottingham Fair and archery contest.	Share and discuss one or two examples of each group's work.
HOUR 4	Recap on the story so far, then continue reading 'The Golden Arrow' from page 74 to end.	Parts of speech cloze activity.	1 & 4: Write 'The Nottingham News' front page for the day. 2 & 3*: Write character study of Maid Marion. *The teacher supports Group 4.	Share and discuss one or two examples of each group's work.
HOUR 5	Recap on the two stories and briefly discuss the book as a whole: cover, design, blurb, illustrations.	Introduce the Book Review sheet and remind pupils of the skills necessary to complete it.	1–4*: All pupils complete a Book Review sheet. Pupils in Group 4 complete just one character and place description if necessary.	Pupils read out and discuss their evaluations in the final section.

RESOURCES

A half-class set of *Robin Hood and the Sheriff* by Julian Atterton, Walker Books (ISBN 0-7445-2490-3), photocopiable pages 179 (Reading Comprehension), 180 (Characters in 'Robin Hood'), 181 (The Nottingham News), 182 (Robin Hood Cloze), 183 (Book Review) and 32 (Useful Character Adjectives) from 'Dustbin Charlie' unit, Term 1, board or flip chart, OHP and acetate (optional), dictionaries, writing materials.

PREPARATION

Prepare enough copies of photocopiable page 179 (Reading Comprehension) for all groups. Prepare enough copies of photocopiable page 180 (Characters in 'Robin Hood') for Groups 1–3, enlarging to A3 size if possible to allow more writing space. (If using the Useful Character Adjectives sheet on page 32 from 'Dustbin Charlie' unit, Term 1, prepare enough copies for all groups.)

Prepare two versions of photocopiable page 181 ('The Nottingham News').

Version 1 is as printed; make enough copies for Group 4 plus a few spares.

Version 2 should have the subheadings deleted; make enough copies for the rest of the class, plus a few spares. Enlarge both versions to A3 size if possible to allow more space for writing.

Make an OHT (or A3 enlargement) of photocopiable page 182 (Robin Hood Cloze). Make an OHT (or A3 enlargement) of photocopiable page 183 (Book Review) and prepare enough copies for the whole class.

SYNOPSIS

The above book, by award-winning author Julian Atterton, contains two adventure stories about Robin Hood and his enemy, the Sheriff of Nottingham. In the first story 'Robin Hood and the Sheriff', Robin Hood performs true to his legendary character when he helps a poor knight who has been unjustly treated by the Sheriff of Nottingham.

In the second story, 'The Golden Arrow', Robin Hood wins the archery contest at the Nottingham Fair only to be then tricked and captured by the Sheriff of Nottingham. But Robin has an unknown friend in the large shape of Friar Tuck. With the help of Maid Marion, the Friar plots Robin's escape and the story ends happily ever after with the wedding of Robin and Marion.

Introduction

Through discussion, establish what the class already know about Robin Hood. Write the important points on the board or flip chart. For example:
■ Legendary English outlaw and popular hero.
■ Born around 1160 at Locksley, Nottinghamshire.
■ Lived in Sherwood Forest because he was outlawed for debt.
■ Known for his personal courage, archery skills, generosity and popularity.
■ Headed a band of men who 'robbed from the rich and gave to the poor'.
■ Had a sweetheart called Maid Marion.
■ Had two friends called Friar Tuck and Little John.

Then read the 'Robin Hood and the Sheriff' story on pages 9 to 30. This will take about 15 minutes.

Whole-class skills work

Identify new and difficult vocabulary in the text, particularly archaic words and phrases, such as: *lone* (page 9); *outlaw, dismounted, forester, bound* (page 10); *thicket, glade* (page 12); *venison* (page 15); *careworn, gallant* (page 16); *inheritance* (page 17), *pledge, harried* (page 18), *rafters* (page 22), *gloat* (page 23), *clenched* (page 26), *flailing* (page 29).

Write the words up on the board or flip chart and use a combination of methods to determine their meaning, for example ask who knows, read the surrounding text to see if it gives clues, check in the dictionary. Add to the list during the course of reading the book.

Differentiated group activities

All children work in pairs within their groups, sharing a copy of the text.
1*: Complete the Characters in 'Robin Hood' sheet. The children can make up their own adjectives or choose appropriate ones from the 'Character Adjectives' sheet from 'Dustbin Charlie' unit, Term 2. When describing the character they should use ideas from the story, but can also refer to the illustrations.
2 & 3: Complete parts A and B of the Reading Comprehension sheet. (Note that this comprehension is differentiated as follows: part A contains simple questions based on Chapter 1 only. Part B contains slightly harder questions based on Chapter 2, and part C contains harder questions based on Chapters 3 and 4.)
4*: Work on part A only of the Reading Comprehension sheet, supported by the teacher.

Conclusion

Explore the key idea in this story about Robin Hood's character. Pose the question: Why did Robin not rob Sir Richard? Aim for the children to gradually work out that Robin's moral code is to take from the rich to help the poor. Sir Richard of Lee is not only poor, but he needs help to save his son.

Introduction

Retell the main events so far in the story of 'Robin Hood and the Sheriff', then read pages 31 to 49. Pause at the end of page 34. Ask the children who they think the man dressed in the potter's apron is. Why? Encourage them to elicit evidence from the text for their responses, then continue reading.

Whole-class skills work

Write on the board or flip chart: 'Ashra took a cup from the shelf and Ashra dropped the cup.' Then write: 'Ashra took a cup from the shelf and she dropped it.' Ask the children to tell you what the difference is. Explain the term 'pronoun': a pronoun is used instead of a noun to avoid needless repetition. With the children, rewrite the first paragraph on page 31 without pronouns. Then ask the children to read out the passage and comment on how it sounds (boring, repetitive, silly!). Ask them to look for examples of the pronouns 'he/she/it' on the first five pages of the day's reading. In each case, the children should say what noun the pronoun is referring to. Establish how pronouns are used to mark gender.

Differentiated group activities

1: Complete all parts of the Comprehension sheet.
2 & 3*: Complete the Characters sheet (see 'Hour 1' for details).
4: Design a 'Wanted' poster for Robin Hood. The poster should contain a description of him.

Conclusion

Continue the discussion about the ideas in the story. Remind the children of yesterday's discussion and ask them: Why did Robin rob the Sheriff? Discuss: Do you agree with Robin's moral code?

Introduction

Read the second story in the book, 'The Golden Arrow' from page 53 to 73. This should take about 15 minutes.

Whole-class skills work

Spend five minutes identifying a small selection of new vocabulary and establishing its meaning, for example *cassock* (page 53), *imploringly* (page 58), *lodged* (page 61), *marksmanship* (page 68), *assent* (page 70). The purpose of this short session is to model for children how they should tackle new words they encounter in independent reading. It is not necessary to establish/look up the meaning of every unknown word. However, dealing with just a few will help them to build up their reading and writing vocabulary.

Revise and build on what was taught about pronouns in Hour 2. Write these pronouns on the board or chart in two columns: Column 1 – *I, you, he, she, it, we, they;* Column 2 – *me, you, him, her, it, us, them.* Choose sentences from the story, write them out and ask the children to identify the pronouns. After several examples, make explicit how the pronouns in Column 1 are used mainly at the beginning of sentences (subject pronouns) and those in Column 2 at the end (object pronouns).

Differentiated group activities

1*: Using the Characters sheet as a model, write a character study of Maid Marion.
2 & 3: Write 'The Nottingham News' for the day, using version 2 of the template (see 'Preparation'). Concentrate on two news items: the archery contest, and the capture of Robin Hood. The children should find and report on as many detailed facts as possible.
4*: Write and design an advertisement for the Nottingham Fair featuring the archery contest. The children should look back through the text so that they can include all the necessary details.

Conclusion

Share and discuss one or two examples of the work of each group. Encourage the rest of the class to listen and evaluate. Ask the children to comment on how many details from the story were used in the newspaper articles, character descriptions and advertisements.

Introduction

Retell the main events so far in the story of 'The Golden Arrow', then continue reading from page 74 to the end. This should take about 15 minutes.

Whole-class skills work

Using an OHT or enlarged version of the cloze activity on photocopiable page 182, revise the basic parts of speech. The photocopiable sheet contains a passage from page 76 of the story. It omits different parts of speech and so draws together knowledge covered previously. Before beginning, it is best to recap on these parts of speech: nouns – 'naming' words; pronouns – replace nouns; adjectives – 'describing' words; verbs – 'doing' words.

Go through the exercise with the children, asking them to suggest appropriate words and filling them in. Accept any words which make sense and which are the correct part of speech. Compare and evaluate the class version of the passage with that in the book.

Differentiated group activities

1: Write 'The Nottingham News' for the day, using version 2 of the template (see 'Preparation' section).
2 & 3*: Using the Characters sheet as a model, write a character study of Maid Marion.
4*: Write 'The Nottingham News' for the day, using the photocopiable template as it stands (version 1). This has subheadings for three main sections and so provides more support for the children's writing.

Conclusion

Share and evaluate one or two examples of each type of work.

Introduction

Explain to the class that now they have finished reading the book, they are going to review it. Recap on the two stories and hold a brief evaluative discussion on the book as a whole: how the 'two-books-in-one' concept works, cover design, blurb, illustrations, the characters that are the same in both stories, the settings that are the same, what quality of adventure these stories offer and so on.

Whole-class skills work

Display the Book Review photocopiable sheet as an OHT or A3 enlargement and explain how to complete it:
■ Write a short summary of the story. (Explain that because this book has two stories in it, the children will need to decide whether to summarize and evaluate just one story, or treat the two stories as one.)
■ Describe one of the characters in the story. Use ideas from the Characters sheet.
■ Describe a place in the story.
■ Write three new words from the story with their meanings.
■ Evaluate the illustrations.
■ Give a star rating to the story/book and explain your reasons for this rating.

Differentiated group activities

Give a copy of the photocopiable Book Review sheet to each child. The teacher should give support where needed in the activities below.
1*: Use the headings on the sheet as a paragraph plan for a review in essay format.
2 & 3*: Use the sheet as it stands.
4*: Write either a character description or a place description if there is insufficient time to complete all sections on the sheet.

Conclusion

Compare and discuss the evaluation sections of the children's Book Review sheets.

READING COMPREHENSION

PART A

Re-read Chapter 1.

- How does Much know that the traveller is a knight?
- What is the traveller's name?
- How much money is in his wallet?
- Where is he going to?
- What has the Sheriff of Nottingham done to his son?
- How does Robin offer to help him?

PART B

Re-read Chapter 2.

- What does the abbot hope to get from Sir Richard?
- What does Sir Richard ask for?
- Who pays the money that he owes?
- When the Sheriff's men-at-arms arrive, what does Little John do?
- How does the Sheriff get his own back at the end of the chapter?

PART C

Re-read Chapters 3 and 4.

- What trick does Robin use to get past the man-at-arms at the gate?
- How does Robin rescue Sir Richard?
- When the Sheriff travels through Sherwood, he is captured by Robin and forced to be a dinner guest. Compare his behaviour with Sir Richard's (see pages 12 to 16).
- How does Robin solve Sir Richard's problem once and for all?

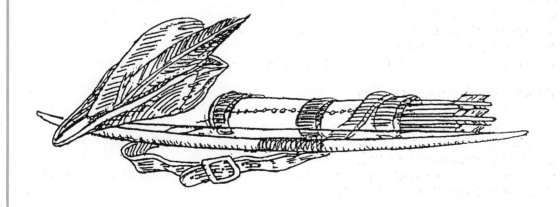

CHARACTERS IN 'ROBIN HOOD'

Who is he?

SIR RICHARD LEE

What is he like?

Choose some adjectives to describe him.

What does he do in the story?

Who is he?

ROBIN HOOD

What is he like?

Choose some adjectives to describe him.

What does he do in the story?

Who is he?

ABBOT OF SAINT MARY'S

What is he like?

Choose some adjectives to describe him.

What does he do in the story?

Who is he?

SHERIFF OF NOTTINGHAM

What is he like?

Choose some adjectives to describe him.

What does he do in the story?

The Nottingham News

THE ARCHERY CONTEST

ROBIN HOOD CAPTURED

ROBIN HOOD ESCAPES

100 LITERACY HOURS ■ YEAR 3 TERM 3

181

ROBIN HOOD CLOZE

Place a word in each of the gaps below. The words in brackets under each gap tell you which part of the speech is needed – (noun, verb, adjective or pronoun).

The jailer on guard in the keep-tower was _____ over
(verb)

the last of his supper when into his chamber walked a

_____ maiden escorted by a friar as fat as a
(adjective)

_____, who held a purse clinking with
(noun)

_____ _____.
(adjective)   (noun)

   "We beg a moment with Robin Hood," he _____.
(verb)

   "This _____ lady is _____ sister come to
(adjective)   (pronoun)

say farewell. I myself have come to hear his confession."

   The jailer held out _____ hand and grinned, and
(pronoun)

when he had stowed the purse in the wallet of his

_____ he rose and _____ a torch at his
(noun)   (verb)

brazier and led them down to _____ vaults hewn deep
(adjective)

into the _____ rock on which the castle stood. He
(adjective)

_____ a door with a _____ from the ring on
(verb)   (noun)

his belt, drew back two bolts and pushed _____ open.
(pronoun)

From page 76 of *Robin Hood and the Sheriff* by Julian Atterton, © Julian Atterton (1995, Walker Books).

BOOK REVIEW

Title of book: _____

Author: _____

Review written by: _____

■ What is the story about?

_____

_____

■ Describe a character from the story.

_____

_____

■ Describe a place in the story.

_____

_____

■ Write down three new words that you learned from the story. Say what they mean.

_____

_____

_____

■ What do you think of the illustrations on the cover and inside the book?

_____

_____

■ How many stars would you give the book and why?
(Key: ☆☆☆☆☆ = couldn't put it down, ☆☆☆☆ = a good read, ☆☆☆ = not bad, ☆☆ = hard work, ☆ = used it to prop up a bookcase.)

_____

PIRATE ADVENTURE

OBJECTIVES

UNIT	SPELLING/VOCABULARY	GRAMMAR/PUNCTUATION	COMPREHENSION/ COMPOSITION
WRITING FICTION Write a story in chapters: 'Pirate adventures'.	Identify misspelled words in own writing. Use synonyms for 'said' and other high-frequency words.	Revise and consolidate key skills learned throughout the year using the Redrafting Checklist as a guide.	Write an episodic story in chapters modelled on known stories.

ORGANIZATION (4 HOURS)

	INTRODUCTION	WHOLE-CLASS SKILLS WORK	DIFFERENTIATED GROUP ACTIVITIES	CONCLUSION
HOUR 1	Examine chaptered stories and investigate structure. Introduce story writing task and look at photocopiable stimulus sheet, modelling how to use it for ideas.	Revise and consolidate use of capital letters.	1–4*: Choose characters to develop from the pictures on the Story Map sheet, and use the map to get ideas for different adventures. Make notes.	Share ideas from the brainstorming session.
HOUR 2	Examine story openings and discuss different ways of beginning a story.	Revise and consolidate conventions of paragraphs.	1–4*: Write or outline first chapter, introducing main characters and settings(s).	Selected pupils read their first chapters. Evaluation.
HOUR 3	Examine chaptered stories. Identify difference between episodic, self-contained chapters and continuation of same story in chapters.	Revise and consolidate punctuation of sentences and speech, and use of apostrophes.	1–4*: Write (or outline) another chapter.	Shared reading of chapters. Pupils write some additional chapters for homework.
HOUR 4	Shared reading of pupils' story with at least three characters. Discuss effectiveness. How do chapters work: continuation of episodic?	Revise and consolidate importance of checking vocabulary and spelling when redrafting.	1–4*: Working with a partner, pupils identify aspects of their stories for redrafting and redraft according to time available.	Discuss the types of things identified for redrafting and evaluate the changes made. Discuss how work may be 'published'.

RESOURCES

Photocopiable pages 188 (Pirate Adventure), 189 (Story Beginnings) and 160 (Redrafting Checklist) from 'Proverbs' unit, a collection of enough short, chaptered stories (including, if possible, *Robin Hood and the Sheriff* from the previous unit) for at least one between three children, board or flip chart, writing materials.

PREPARATION

Photocopy enough of all the above photocopiable sheets for one between two. If possible, prepare an OHT of the photocopiable page 189 (Story Beginnings), or enlarge to A3.

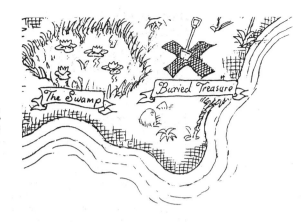

Introduction

Distribute copies of the chaptered books you have collected, so that there is one for at least two or three children. Ask them to leaf through them and discuss how they are organized. Make sure they understand the term 'chapter'. Look at the variety of ways chapters are indicated, for example by number, by chapter title, by both.

Next, introduce the writing task, explaining to the children that they are going to write a pirate adventure in chapters, based on the pictures and map on photocopiable page 188 (Pirate Adventure). Look at this sheet with the children and explain how to use it as a basis for ideas by modelling the process, for example choose a main character and give him/her a name. Then choose companions for the character. Tell how these characters become shipwrecked on the island and so on.

Whole-class skills work

Revise and consolidate the use of capital letters on part 2, section 1 of the Redrafting Checklist (page 160):

CAPITAL LETTERS
Have you used capital letters for:
■ beginning sentences?
■ names?
■ places?
■ days, months, special occasions?
Do this orally by asking the children for examples and getting them to write these on the board, followed by asking the rest of the class 'Is that correct?'

Differentiated group activities

1–4*: All groups work to plan their story, using the Pirate Adventure photocopiable sheet (page 188) as a stimulus. Children in Group 1 might write individual stories, while those in Groups 2 and 3 could write in pairs. Group 4 should write a group story. In all cases though, groups should be encouraged to share their ideas.

The children should start by choosing the characters they wish to develop from the photocopiable sheet (as they did for the 'Beat the Bully' unit, Term 1). They can divide a piece of paper into four sections, one for each character, then jot down notes about each character – name, age, gender, background, main character traits and so on. Next, they use the map on the photocopiable sheet to get ideas for different adventures and make notes on these. Finally, they should discuss their characters and adventures with group members and refine their notes further.

Conclusion

The children share ideas from the above session and read out their notes. Encourage them to develop their own notes from any ideas they have picked out from the discussion as a piece of homework.

Introduction

Review previous work on opening paragraphs, for example the 'Beat the Bully' unit (page 33, Term 1), which explored beginning with a description of a character, and look at some different ways of beginning a story, including:
■ description of a place or person
■ dialogue
■ writing in the 1st person – 'I'
■ beginning with an exciting event.
Read the opening paragraphs on the Story Beginnings photocopiable sheet (page 189), displayed as an OHT if possible. Discuss what kind of beginning they are and invite the children to speculate about what might happen next.

Whole-class skills work

Revise and consolidate the use of paragraphs in part 2, section 2 of the Redrafting Checklist photocopiable (page 160):

PARAGRAPHS
Have you:
■ indented the first line of a paragraph?
■ remembered not to leave whole blank lines between paragraphs?
■ started a new paragraph for a new topic, or a new scene in a story?
   Explain that each chapter of the story will be written in several paragraphs. The first chapter will be particularly important as it will introduce the main characters and the setting.

Differentiated group activities

1–4*: Write the beginning of Chapter 1 using one of the types of beginning paragraphs explored earlier. Then continue the chapter to introduce the main characters and setting, and the first adventure.

Conclusion

Selected children read out their first chapters, followed by evaluation. The evaluation should take the form of a discussion about the following:
■ How attention-grabbing and effective is the first paragraph?
■ Does the first chapter introduce the main characters and setting in a way that is interesting and clear?
■ Did you enjoy the first adventure?

Introduction

Examine again the collection of chaptered books. By skimming and scanning, explore the content of chapters, leading to the conclusion that, in some books, chapters break up one story into different parts, whereas in others, chapters include different self-contained episodes or adventures. This may most easily be explained by referring to popular TV soaps. Each performance is described as an 'episode' because the characters and setting are the same – only the story changes. Stories in an episode do not have to follow on one from another (although sometimes they do). The Robin Hood stories are another good example of episodic stories. So, the chapters for the children's pirate adventures can be separate stories using the same characters and setting.

Whole-class skills work

Revise and consolidate punctuation and apostrophes in part 2, sections 3 and 4 of the Redrafting Checklist photocopiable sheet:

PUNCTUATION
Have you:
- used a full stop at the end of sentences?
- used question marks at the end of questions?
- used speech marks before and after words actually spoken?
- begun speech with a capital letter?
- placed a comma, full stop, question mark or exclamation mark before final speech marks?

APOSTROPHES
Have you:
- used an apostrophe to show missing letters in contractions?
- used an apostrophe after a name to show ownership?

Differentiated group activities

1–4*: Write (or outline) another chapter following the guidance given in the introduction. Support children in Group 4 by further discussing the map and how some of the places suggest ideas for other adventures or episodes.

Conclusion

Encourage all the children to write (or outline) some additional chapters for homework.

Introduction

Choose a child's story with three or more chapters and ask that child to read his/her work to the class. Revise the term 'episodic' and discuss whether it applies to the story.

Whole-class skills work

Revise and consolidate the vocabulary and spelling items in part 2, sections 5 and 6 of the Redrafting Checklist. (This session is not intended as a review of spelling rules, it is simply to encourage the children to work in pairs to check the spelling of their stories.)

VOCABULARY
Have you:
- used some interesting adjectives?
- used some synonyms for 'said'?

SPELLING
Have you:
- checked your spelling?

Differentiated group activities

1–4*: Working with a partner, as explained on the Redrafting Checklist, the children redraft their adventure stories. Pupils of different abilities should be given different versions of the Redrafting Checklist which include just enough of the appropriate items to challenge them to improve.

Conclusion

Discuss the types of changes the children have made to their stories. Give particular praise to changes made in part 1 (which focuses on content), as these are often overlooked in favour of mere 'proofreading' changes. Discuss ways of 'publishing' the stories, and suggest that the children could do this as homework (or provide time outside the hour for them to do it).

FURTHER IDEA

Look at characters and settings in other adventure stories: *Treasure Island*, *Robinson Crusoe*, *The Swiss Family Robinson*.

PIRATE ADVENTURE

STORY BEGINNINGS

There are many ways of starting a written story, for example with:

- a description of a place or person
- dialogue
- writing in the 1st person ('I')
- an exiting event.

Look at these beginnings of well-known books and decide which kind of beginning it is. What is it about the beginning that makes you want to read on? When you have done this, try out some different beginnings for your Pirate Adventure story.

* * * * * * * * * * *

Mary Lennox was a spoilt, rude and bad-tempered child. She was never really well, and she was thin and miserable, with a sour face. No one liked her at all.
(*The Secret Garden*, Frances Hodgson Burnett)

Dark spruce forest frowned on either side of the frozen waterway. The trees had been stripped by a recent wind of their white covering of frost, and they seemed to lean toward each other, black and ominous, in the fading light. A vast silence reigned over the land.
(*White Fang*, Jack London)

'Look out, Willie – the canal...!' Super Gran yelled, as she Super-sprinted across the uneven cobblestones of the towpath towards the boy, her grandson Willard, to save him from a watery grave.
(*Super Gran Rules OK!*, Forrest Wilson)

A long time ago, when I was young, on a Wednesday afternoon, a very strange thing happened to me. So strange, you probably won't believe it. That's up to you. Anyway, this is what happened.
(*Princess by Mistake*, Penelope Lively)

Deep in the night, thunder crashed in the dark, leaden skies over Transylvania. Brilliant flashes of fork lightening lit up the jagged mountain and the wicked, hideously shaped Castle Duckula, which perched precariously on its summit.
(*Duckula and the Ghost Train Mystery*, John Broadhead)

I'm going shopping in the village,' George's mother said to George on Saturday morning. 'So be a good boy and don't get up to mischief.' This was a silly thing to say to a small boy at any time. It immediately made him wonder what sort of mischief he might get up to.
(*George's Marvellous Medicine*, Roald Dahl)

WRITING A MAGAZINE

OBJECTIVES

UNIT	SPELLING/VOCABULARY	GRAMMAR/PUNCTUATION	COMPREHENSION/ COMPOSITION
WRITING SIMULATION A magazine.	Correct spelling in proofreading exercise.	Redraft writing with attention to grammar and punctuation.	Recognize the distinctive features of magazines for young people and write own magazine. Explore letter-writing conventions. Revise skills for article, review and story writing.

ORGANIZATION (5 HOURS)

	INTRODUCTION	WHOLE-CLASS SKILLS WORK	DIFFERENTIATED GROUP ACTIVITIES	CONCLUSION
HOUR 1	Look at a range of magazines for the under-tens age group. Identify the different kinds of writing, eg articles, stories, letters, reviews. Read some examples of letters.	Learn letter-writing conventions.	1–4: Write a letter. *The teacher supports Groups 1 & 4.	Selected pupils read out their letters. Evaluate the format of these.
HOUR 2	Read some examples of magazine articles.	Revise structures for information writing (see photocopiable page 172 from 'Words in Windows' unit) and persuasive writing (see photocopiable page 102 from 'Book Token' unit).	1–4: Write a short article. *The teacher supports Groups 2 & 3 in guided writing session.	Selected pupils read out their articles.
HOUR 3	Read an example of a magazine story.	Revise structures for story writing (see photocopiable page 95 (Story Planner) from the 'Myth-maker' unit).	1–4: Write a short story. *The teacher supports Group 4 in a guided writing session.	Selected pupils read out their stories.
HOUR 4	Read some examples of reviews of books, films, CDs etc.	Revise structures for reviews (see photocopiable page 183 (Book Review) from 'Robin Hood' unit).	1–4: Write a review. *The teacher supports Groups 2 & 3.	Selected pupils read out their reviews.
HOUR 5	Look at the different design features of a selection of magazines.	In pairs, proofread and correct the week's work (see photocopiable page 160 (Redrafting Checklist) from 'Proverbs' unit).	1–4*: Design a magazine-style cover for the week's work.	Final products are discussed and evaluated.

RESOURCES

A collection of magazines read by the under-ten age group (ask the children to bring them in), the following photocopiable pages from other units: 108 (Class Rules template) from the 'Rules Rule!' unit, Term 2, 172 (Words in Windows template) from the 'Words in Windows' unit, 95 (Story Planner) from the 'Myth-makers' unit, Term 2, 183 (Book Review) from the 'Robin Hood' unit, 102 (Book Token advert) from the 'Book Token' unit, Term 2 and 160 (Redrafting Checklist) from the 'Proverbs' unit, enough writing materials for all writing throughout the week, including one sheet of A3 paper per child, board or flip chart, OHP and acetate (optional), drawing materials.

PREPARATION

Look through the magazines brought in by the children and ensure that they contain examples of everything you need for the week's work on this unit. Copy enough of the above photocopiable sheets for one between two children. You may also wish to prepare an OHT of the letter template described below in the 'Whole-class skills work' section.

Introduction

Display a selection of the magazines brought in by the children. These will range from special interest magazines, for example horses, games, computer magazines and so on, to general interest magazines. Ask the children who have brought in the examples you have chosen to show their magazines and talk about the content and format of these. Show the covers and comment on the range of articles, the style and the presentation. Make a list of the different types of writing that can be found, ensuring that your list includes letters, reports or information articles, fiction and reviews.

Next, explain that each pair of children is going to produce their own mini-magazine, step by step, throughout the week. Their first task will be to write a letter. Read some examples of letters from the magazines that have been written for a variety of purposes, for example to recount, comment, complain, seek advice and so on.

Whole-class skills work

Explain that letters published in magazines have been edited and so do not always appear in the same format as they were originally written in. However, there is a special layout to follow when writing letters which helps to make them easier to read. Write the following personal letter template on the board or chart (or display it as an OHT) and explain the letter-writing conventions and the punctuation:

Investigate which items of this format have been edited out of the letters that appear in the magazines. Ask the children why they think these items have been left out.

Differentiated group activities

General Note: The children should work in pairs within their ability groups throughout the whole five hours of this unit, producing a magazine between them. This will entail deciding how they share out the writing between partners and, in some cases, you will need to make this decision.

1–4: All groups write a letter for their magazine. This could be a letter to the editor expressing an opinion, a problem-page letter, or a letter offering information. The children should decide on the content. In the case of a problem-page letter, the child and/or the partner, could also write a reply.

*The teacher gives support to children in Groups 1 and 4.

Conclusion

Selected children read out and display their letters. Ensure that they have used letter-writing conventions correctly as part of a brief evaluation session.

HOUR 2

Introduction

Read some examples of short articles from the magazines. Try to include an information article, for example a piece describing a holiday resort or a new product – and a persuasive article which argues a point of view, for example why exercise is good for you.

Whole-class skills work

Since much of the work in this unit is the revision and application of previous skills, templates and checklists from earlier in the year will be reused. For this session, use the photocopiable Words in Windows template from the 'Words in Windows' unit (page 172) and the Book Token Advert photocopiable sheet from the 'Book Token' unit (page 102) as a basis for the revision of skills for writing information texts and persuasive texts.

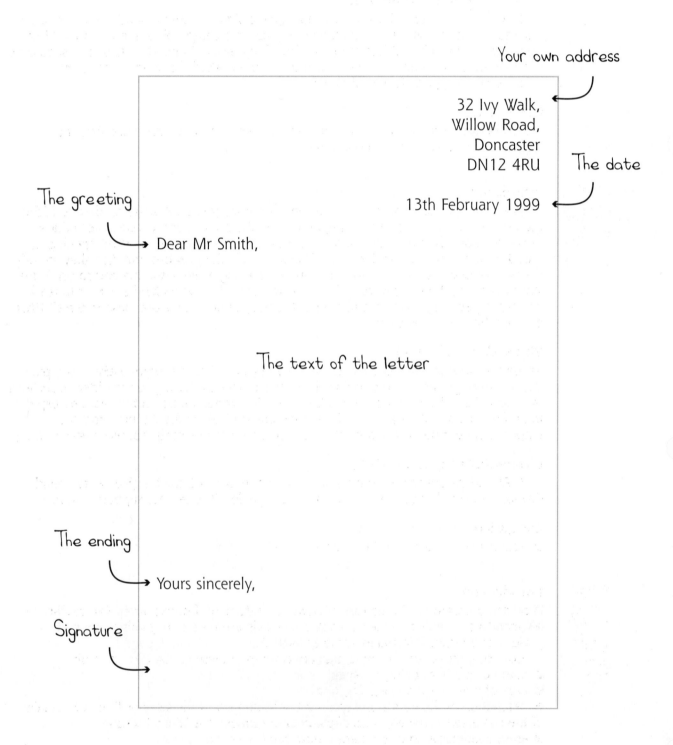

Your own address

32 Ivy Walk,
Willow Road,
Doncaster
DN12 4RU

The date

13th February 1999

The greeting

Dear Mr Smith,

The text of the letter

The ending

Yours sincerely,

Signature

Remind the children that information texts:
- are usually written in the present tense
- focus on a specific subject
- organize the information so it is easy to follow
- support facts with examples, description and explanations.

Remind them that persuasive texts:
- are also usually written in the present tense
- often use the imperative (command) form of the verb
- talk directly to the reader
- say what the benefits are to the reader
- use language and pictures that create memorable images.

Support these points with examples from the magazines you have selected.

Differentiated group activities

1–4: All groups write a short article. More able children should be encouraged to write a persuasive article, using the Class Rules template as a paragraph guide (from the 'Rules Rule!' unit, page 108). Other children (some from Group 3 and all of Group 4) should be encouraged to write an information article using the Words in Windows template. *The teacher supports Groups 2 and 3.

Conclusion

Select some children to share their articles, reading them out with expression and intonation. Evaluate their effectiveness.

Introduction

Read an example of a short story from one of the magazines. Ask the children to identify the beginning, middle and end. Depending on the content of the story, elicit critical responses from the class. The children could assess how effective the story opening is, based on their previous work on Story Beginnings in the previous unit. Can they identify the type of opening, for example description, exciting event, dialogue and so on. Is the story written in the first person – 'I'? How well does the text make them want to read on? Is the pace kept up in the middle of the story or do the children lose interest? What do they think of the ending?

Whole-class skills work

Revise the story-writing skills using the Story Planner from the 'Myth-maker' unit, page 95). Go through the different points listed on the sheet, referring to the different sections of a story. Refer back to the children's own stories written earlier in the year and explore the different ways of beginning, developing and ending stories. At this stage, the emphasis should be on the content rather than the proofreading aspects of story writing.

Differentiated group activities

1–4: All the groups write a short story. Children in Group 1 can be given a free hand. Groups 2–4 should use the Story Planner as a guide. *The teacher supports Group 4.

Conclusion

Selected children read out their stories.

Introduction

Read some examples of magazine reviews of a selection of books, films, CDs and so on, comparing any similar elements. Look at the style used – are they written in the first person, or are they information-style accounts?

Produce a list of similar points that are covered in these reviews, for example:
- name of the item being reviewed
- type of item – is it a story, CD, film?
- description of the item's contents – a brief summary of the story or film plot, details of the characters involved, titles of some of the songs on a CD and so on
- an evaluation/rating of the item – how good is it?

Whole-class skills work

Use the Book Review photocopiable sheet (from the 'Robin Hood' unit, page 183) as a template for writing any kind of review. Talk through the different aspects of the sheet with the children, explaining how each heading can represent a separate part of the review. (For more able children who want to review items other than books or films, suggest that they replace the character and place sections with details of the group/ singer and a favourite track.)

Differentiated group activities

1–4: All groups write reviews. Only the more able children should write reviews of anything other than films or books since this will mean departing from the format of the Book Review sheet. If they prefer, they can use the list produced in the 'Introduction' section instead of the photocopiable sheet as the basis for their review format. Children in Group 4 should be encouraged to write a book review directly onto the Book Review sheet. *The teacher supports Groups 2 and 3.

Conclusion

Selected children read out their reviews.

Introduction

Explain the design features of some of the magazines, looking closely at the covers.

Whole-class skills work

One important task of any magazine publisher is proofreading. Pupils should work in pairs to proofread and correct each other's work using the Redrafting Checklist (page 160) from the 'Proverbs' unit.

Differentiated group activities

1–4*: Unfortunately, it would take far too long to redraft and present all the pieces written throughout the week, however, children can design a cover for their work to make a satisfying finished product. All groups design a cover for their magazine on folded A3 paper. The week's work is then stapled inside.

Conclusion

Evaluate and discuss the final products. Are they interesting to read? Will the cover make people want to look inside?

FURTHER IDEAS

Swap the magazines around so that children can write reviews of each other's magazines. Use star ratings (see Book Review sheets) and total the stars to see which are the most popular magazines.

LIBRARY CLASSIFICATION SYSTEM

OBJECTIVES

UNIT	SPELLING/VOCABULARY	GRAMMAR/PUNCTUATION	COMPREHENSION/COMPOSITION
REFERENCE AND RESEARCH SKILLS Library classification system.	Develop vocabulary related to library usage.	To understand and use a classification code.	To understand library classification systems and use to locate books.

ORGANIZATION (1 HOUR)

INTRODUCTION	WHOLE-CLASS SKILLS WORK	DIFFERENTIATED GROUP ACTIVITIES	CONCLUSION
Classify a collection of books as fiction or non-fiction. Identify purpose of library label on book spines. Read photocopiable text about the library classification system.	Use the information from the text to give library labels to unlabelled books.	1–4*: All groups take turns to visit the library and carry out differentiated activities to develop knowledge of classification system. Classroom classification activity.	Review work done in classroom classification activity.

RESOURCES

A collection of fiction and non-fiction books from the school library with classification labels on their spine, a collection of fiction and non-fiction books that are not classified (perhaps from the class library – colour-coded books are acceptable), access to the school library, photocopiable page 197 (How Books are Classified in the Library), writing materials.

PREPARATION

Collect together some fiction and non-fiction books that are labelled from the school library. Also collect some that are not labelled. Ensure that you can have access to the school library for the hour. Make enough copies of photocopiable page 197 for one between two and, if possible, make an OHT or enlarged A3 copy of it.

Introduction

Display the collection of books from the school library and ask the children to classify them as fiction or non-fiction. You may need to start by revising the meaning of 'fiction' and 'non-fiction'. Ensure also that the children understand the terms 'classify' and 'classification'. Then ask them if there is any other information on the books that might help in classifying them. Direct their attention to the spines of the books and the special letters and numbers on them. Do they know what they are? Display photocopiable page 197 on the OHP if possible and read the text.

Whole-class skills work

Hold up examples of fiction and non-fiction books that are not labelled and ask the children to suggest how they should be labelled. Do enough to satisfy yourself that they understand the classification system.

Differentiated group activities

Give each pair of children a copy of the library classification system text on photocopiable page 196. Take all four groups in turn to visit the school library to look at how the books are organized. Set them tasks to find different books, tailoring the 'hunt' to the children's ability, for example:

1*: Find a book on whales by Donald Smith. Find *The Sheep-Pig* by Dick King-Smith.

2 & 3*: Find a book on whales. Find a book by Roald Dahl (or any other author that they will recognize as a fiction writer).

4*: Find a history book. Find a fiction book.

When they are not in the library, the children should use the photocopiable sheet as a reference to classify other books in the classroom. Ask them to write down the title of the book and the author, and then give it a classification label. They could do this in a grid format.

Conclusion

Select pairs of children to present their book classifications to the others. Discuss whether these are correct or not, and ensure that the children have grasped the library classification system.

HOW BOOKS ARE CLASSIFIED IN THE LIBRARY

Have you ever noticed the letters and numbers on the spines of library books? Do you know what they mean and how to use them?

The books in a library are either fiction or non-fiction. **Fiction books** are in a separate section from non-fiction books. Fiction books are made-up stories about people, places or things. They are arranged on the shelves in alphabetical order, using the author's last name. On the spine of a fiction book you will see:

- the title of the book
- the author's surname
- the initial letter of the author's first name.

If two authors have the same last name, look at the first name.
If there are two or more books by the same author, they are arranged in alphabetical order by titles.
If the title of a book begins with *a*, *an* or *the*, alphabetize by the second word of the title.

BRING ME A RAINBOW	THE SCHOOL PARTY	THE DANCING PENCIL	JENNY'S JOURNEY
Roberts A ▲	Smith B ▲	Smith R ▲	Williams J ▲

Non-fiction books contain facts about all kinds of subjects. All non-fiction books in the library have numbers *and* letters on their spines. As with fiction books, the letters on non-fiction books are the first letters of the authors' names. The numbers are taken from a plan called the Dewey Decimal System. This was invented in 1876 by a man named Melvil Dewey. He thought it would help libraries organize their books better if each book had a number according to what it was about. In that way, all books about the same subject would be near each other on the shelf.

In Mr Dewey's system, all non-fiction books are divided into ten main subject groups. Here is a chart of the system:

SET NUMBER	GROUP NAME	WHAT THE BOOKS ARE ABOUT
000–999	General works	Many different subjects
100–199	Philosophy	People's thoughts and their ways of thinking
200–299	Religion	People's ideas about God
300–399	Social sciences	How people live together
400–499	Language	How people talk to each other
500–599	Pure science	Nature, the world and the universe
600–699	Technology (Applied science)	Ways to use science to help us
700–799	The arts	Painting, music, dancing, sports and games
800–899	Literature	Stories and poetry
900–999	History Geography Biography	People, places and important events

Because each of these 10 main groups deals with a lot of information, each group is divided again into 10 groups. Do you see why it is called the Dewey *Decimal* System?

CONVERSATION AT THE SCHOOL DINNER TABLE

OBJECTIVES

UNIT	SPELLING/VOCABULARY	GRAMMAR/PUNCTUATION	COMPREHENSION/ COMPOSITION
WORD PLAY 'Conversation at the school dinner table' by John Rice.	Read nonsense words by phonic knowledge and by breaking down into syllables.	Investigate a humorous, alternative way of depicting speech.	Explore humour through word play.

ORGANIZATION (4 HOURS)

	INTRODUCTION	WHOLE-CLASS SKILLS WORK	DIFFERENTIATED GROUP ACTIVITIES	CONCLUSION
HOUR 1	Share the poem. Discuss how the poem is structured and how humour is achieved.	Examine nonsense words and decode using phonic knowledge and by breaking down into syllables.	1: Rewrite poem as conversation using speech marks. 2 & 3*: Read poem aloud, each pupil taking a verse in turn. 4*: Practise reading nonsense words. Read poem with teacher.	Class divides into groups representing speakers in poem and re-reads appropriate verses.

RESOURCES

Photocopiable page 200 ('Conversation at the School Dinner Table'), board or flip chart, OHP and acetate (optional), writing materials.

PREPARATION

If possible, prepare the poem on page 200 as an OHT. Otherwise, enlarge it to A3. Make enough copies for one per child. Prepare the reading of the poem – it's a tricky one!

Introduction

Read out the poem to the class, emphasizing the conversation format, the different voices and the nonsense words. Display the poem and read it again with the children following. Ask the children why they think the poem is funny. Help them to see that it is not simply the nonsense words that provide the humour, but the fact that *some* of the words are ones we actually use (ask which ones) and that informal conversations often do sound like this. Look at the structure of the poem to establish that each verse represents a different person speaking.

Whole-class skills work

Give each child a copy of the poem so that they can investigate it more closely. The poem contains twelve nonsense words (although it looks like more!). Write them on the board or flip chart. Ask someone to read the first one – 'thingummyjiggery'. If the child reads it correctly, ask how he/she tackled it. (The answer will, undoubtedly, be by breaking it down into syllables and sounding it out.) If the child does not read it correctly, suggest using the syllable method, then ask another child to come up to the board and divide the word up – 'thin/gum/my/jig/ger/y'. How many syllables are there? Do the same with the other words.

Differentiated group activities

1: Look at the poem and determine how many speakers there are. (It could be three or four.) Give each speaker a name. Then write the poem out as a conversation using speech marks and 'said xxx' for each speaker.
2 & 3*: In smaller sub-groups, read the poem aloud, taking it in turns to read the verses. The children should be encouraged to read with appropriate expression and intonation.
4*: Practise reading the nonsense words. Then read the poem with the teacher's support, each child taking a verse in turn.

Conclusion

Ask members of Group 1 how many speakers they decided that the poem featured. Agree on this issue as a class. Then divide the class into that number of groups and re-read the poem, with each group taking the part of one speaker.

CONVERSATION AT THE SCHOOL DINNER TABLE

Could you please pass the
    Thingummyjiggery
    Whatchamacallit
    Whojamaflippery
    Thingummybob.

What? Do you mean the
    Whangeebangee
    Woobbleyboobley
    Whiffleyspiffley
    Sooperydoop?

No, I mean the
    Thingummyjiggery
    Whatchamacallit
    Whojamaflippery
    Thingummybob.

Oh, the
    Thingummyjiggery
    Whatchamacallit
    Whojamaflippery
    Thingummybob.

Yes, the
    Thingummyjiggery
    Whatchamacallit
    Whojamaflippery
    Thingummybob.

Give the
    Whangeebangee
    Woobbleyboobley
    Whiffleyspiffley
    Sooperydoop
to whatsisname.

I don't want the
    Whangeebangee
    Woobbleyboobley
    Whiffleyspiffley
    Sooperydoop.

I want the
    Pranzocranzo
    Figgledekoop
    Jaunterysauntery
    Zogledezoop.

What do you want with the
    Pranzocranzo
    Figgledekoop
    Jaunterysauntery
    Zogledezoop?

I pour it all over my
    Thingummyjiggery
    Whatchamacallit
    Whojamaflippery
    Thingummybob.

John Rice

Follow-up

DUSTBIN CHARLIE CLEANS UP

OBJECTIVES

UNIT	SPELLING/VOCABULARY	GRAMMAR/PUNCTUATION	COMPREHENSION/ COMPOSITION
READING FICTION Sequel: *Dustbin Charlie Cleans Up* by Ann Pilling.	Extend vocabulary from text. Investigate compound words. Spell *oi* words (noise, oil).	Practise skills from previous unit (adjectives, nouns, capital letters). Use of capitalized and italicized print in text.	Recognize and identify consistency of setting and characters in sequel. Compare story openings. Understand and discuss plot; prediction.

ORGANIZATION (5 HOURS)

	INTRODUCTION	WHOLE-CLASS SKILLS WORK	DIFFERENTIATED GROUP ACTIVITIES	CONCLUSIONS
HOUR 1	Introduce sequel and recall characters and setting. Read first chapter. Discuss: Who is Mildred?	Identify adjectives. Explore use of capitalized and italicized print in text.	1*: Write comparative description of settings from illustrations (farm – pages 8–9 in first book; Union Street – pages 10–11 in sequel). 2 & 3: Write detailed description of Union Street. 4*: Re-read first chapter, followed by discussion, all with teacher.	Share selected descriptions and sum up story so far.
HOUR 2	Read second chapter. Confirm/discard predictions about Mildred.	Identify nouns.	1: Describe how Grandad and Charlie each feel about Mildred. 2 & 3*: Re-read chapter as play, with narrator and dialogue of characters. 4: Activity based on compound words.	Look at title of next chapter. Discuss what shock might be.
HOUR 3	Confirm/discard predictions about shock. Read third chapter.	Explore compound words – headlamp, outside, carwash.	1*: Write about own 'nightmare'. 2 & 3: Cloze based on carwash scene. 4*: Re-read description of carwash. Discuss Charlie's feelings and relate to own experience.	Recap story so far, focusing on Charlie's feelings. Elicit personal response to story.
HOUR 4	Read to page 71. Discuss: How will Charlie clean Tin Man? Read to end of chapter.	Revise capital letters for names, places, days. Spelling of *oi* words such as oil, noise.	1: Read chapter as a play. 2 & 3*: Write about what is happening on pages 80–81. 4: Cloze based on second car wash scene (pages 78–84).	Compare with first book. Share ideas for sequel story lines and evaluate.
HOUR 5	Discuss how story works both as stand alone and as sequel.	Look at book features (front and back covers, blurb, author details etc). Teach/revise 'book talk' vocabulary.	1–4: Discuss ideas for sequel, based on Charlie and Tin Man and set on farm. Teacher supports where necessary.	Discuss: would new characters need to be introduced?

DEEP WATER

OBJECTIVES

UNIT	SPELLING/VOCABULARY	GRAMMAR/PUNCTUATION	COMPREHENSION/ COMPOSITION
READING FICTION Historical fiction: Chapter 4 'Deep Water' from *On the Banks of Plum Creek* by Laura Ingalls Wilder.	Spell words with double consonants.		Compare two related pieces of writing. Understand the difference between fact and fiction.

ORGANIZATION (1 HOUR)

	INTRODUCTION	WHOLE-CLASS SKILLS WORK	DIFFERENTIATED GROUP ACTIVITIES	CONCLUSION
HOUR 1	Read Chapter 4 'Deep Water', from *On the Banks of Plum Creek*. Relate to the extract from *Searching for Laura Ingalls*. Explore the difference between fact and fiction. *On the Banks of Plum Creek* is a fictionalized account of the author's childhood in frontier America (written as story in 3rd person, past tense).	Use text as basis for work on reading and spelling words with double consonants: *dresses, cattle, willow, grassy, tall* and so on.	1: Discuss Laura's 'thrill of fear' writing. Write personal account relating to own experience. 2 & 3*: Examine paragraphs 2 and 5. Explore effect of specific adjectives to describe setting. 4: Spelling work to reinforce previous session.	Select one or two children from Group 1 to read their accounts. Ask one or two others in class to relate their own experiences. Suggest these ideas could be used to write fictional stories – in another writing session or at home.

(SEE 'DIARY WRITING', PAGE 49)

ACROSTIC VARIATIONS

OBJECTIVES

UNIT	SPELLING/VOCABULARY	GRAMMAR/PUNCTUATION	COMPREHENSION/ COMPOSITION
WRITING POETRY Variations on the acrostic format.	Use the correct spelling of known words as the basis for writing a poem.	Understand the difference between a phrase and a sentence.	Understand a specific poetic format and write from a model.

ORGANIZATION (1 HOUR)

	INTRODUCTION	WHOLE-CLASS SKILLS WORK	DIFFERENTIATED GROUP ACTIVITIES	CONCLUSION
HOUR 1	Read 'School Daze' and 'Bulb' on photocopiable page 61. Explain that 'School Daze' is a 'centre acrostic'. (These have to be carefully planned, because if the first part of the line is more than two words, the visual effect is lost.) 'Bulb' is a 'riddle acrostic' (designed by indenting alternate lines). The content should describe the subject of the riddle but without using the actual word or giving away the subject too easily.	Use examples on the photocopiable sheet to demonstrate that lines do not need to be complete sentences. Explore the difference between phrases and sentences.	1–3: Develop acrostic writing using these variations on the acrostic format as models. 4*: Ensure that pupils in this group are confident in writing simple acrostics before trying acrostic variations.	Share selected poems and discuss how best the poems could be collected together in a class anthology.

PANDORA'S BOX 2

(SEE 'PANDORA'S BOX', PAGE 82)

OBJECTIVES

UNIT	SPELLING/VOCABULARY	GRAMMAR/PUNCTUATION	COMPREHENSION/ COMPOSITION
READING FICTION Myths and Legends: Comparing versions of 'Pandora's Box.'			Understand why there are different versions of the story. Compare versions, looking at characters, plot and setting.

ORGANIZATION (1 HOUR)

INTRODUCTION	WHOLE-CLASS SKILLS WORK	DIFFERENTIATED GROUP ACTIVITIES	CONCLUSION
Collect other versions of the 'Pandora's Box' myth and show the children the variety. Depending on the length of these versions, choose one or two to read aloud.	Compare the versions of the story using a 'same/ different' column grid.	1: Read independently another version of the story and make a comparison grid. 2 & 3*: Read another version of the story with the teacher and discuss similarities and differences. 4: In pairs, and using a tape recorder, tell their version of the story.	Discuss the different versions. Pupils express personal responses and give reasons.

HOUR 1

A COLLECTION OF MYTHS AND LEGENDS

OBJECTIVES

UNIT	SPELLING/VOCABULARY	GRAMMAR/PUNCTUATION	COMPREHENSION/ COMPOSITION
WRITING FICTION Myths and Legends: Publishing a class collection of myths and legends.	Check the spelling of uncertain words for the redraft of their stories.	Redraft stories to the agreed format and incorporate correct grammar and punctuation.	Explore examples of collections and anthologies to see their features. Redraft and present final version of their story to the agreed format for a class collection.

ORGANIZATION (1 HOUR)

	INTRODUCTION	WHOLE-CLASS SKILLS WORK	DIFFERENTIATED GROUP ACTIVITIES	CONCLUSION
HOUR 1	Collect a number of story anthologies, including myths and legends. Explore the features of a collection – eg cover details such as title, illustration, 'blurb'; internal layout and design (eg the stories are different, but are probably laid out the same, with the same illustrator throughout).	Make a list of the various features that need to be agreed for a class collection. Then agree them – eg What will the title be? Will the stories be on lined or unlined paper? Will the first letter of each story be a large, coloured one? Will there be illustrations? If so, will they be in black and white or colour? And so on.	1–4*: All groups finish off their stories according to the agreed format. The teacher provides support as necessary.	Publish the stories by binding them into a cover. Give each group a different task – eg front cover, back cover, contents, page etc.

INSTRUCTIONS AND DIRECTIONS

OBJECTIVES

UNIT	SPELLING/VOCABULARY	GRAMMAR/PUNCTUATION	COMPREHENSION/ COMPOSITION
READING NON-FICTION Procedural genre: Instructions and directions.	Spell sequence words.	Recognize sequence words and phrases, and layout devices that indicate sequence.	Identify and discuss a range of purposes of instructions and directions.

ORGANIZATION (1 HOUR)

INTRODUCTION	WHOLE-CLASS SKILLS WORK	DIFFERENTIATED GROUP ACTIVITIES	CONCLUSION
Display and discuss real-life examples of directions and instructions that have been brought into class (recipes, how to use a product, how to get from one place to another, how to play a game, etc).	Reorder various out-of-order sequence words: eg finally, first, next; finish by, now, start by, the third step is... etc. Make a class poster listing the features of good procedural writing which can be used as an aide-memoire.	1*: Work in pairs reading and evaluating real-life examples of instructions/ directions. 2 & 3: Sequencing activities using cup-up versions of real-life examples of instructions. 4*: As above, with simplified text.	Select pupils from each group to present what they have done and discuss their work. Reiterate features of procedural writing with reference to the class poster.

A NECKLACE OF RAINDROPS

OBJECTIVES

UNIT	SPELLING/VOCABULARY	GRAMMAR/PUNCTUATION	COMPREHENSION/COMPOSITION
READING FICTION AND POETRY Short stories: *A Necklace of Raindrops* by Joan Aiken.	Spell words with the suffix *-ing*; introduce doubling consonants rule. Investigate compound words. Spell the days of the week. Develop vocabulary from reading. Use a dictionary and a thesaurus.	Compare adjectives. Revise the use of capital letters. Identify and use sequencing words. Predict words from the grammatical context.	Develop basic reading skills. Make predictions. Identify themes. Discuss and map out plots. Fact *versus* fiction. Appreciate the figurative use of language.

ORGANIZATION (5 HOURS)

	INTRODUCTION	WHOLE-CLASS SKILLS WORK	DIFFERENTIATED GROUP ACTIVITIES	CONCLUSION
HOUR 1	Read 'The Elves in the Shelves' on page 56, up to the question on page 57. Invite prediction. Then read to end and check predictions.	Use the description of book creatures on pages 57–58 to revise spelling of *-ing* suffix. Teach doubling consonant rule.	1*: Skim re-read of story. Discuss what could and could not have really happened. 2 & 3: Skills activity based on comparative and superlative adjectives. 4*: Discuss which book characters pupils would like to play with and why.	Groups 1 & 4 share their ideas to generate class discussion.
HOUR 2	Read 'The Three Travellers' on pages 69–81.	Use words from story (eg: 'railway', 'signalman', 'paperweight', 'skyscraper') to investigate and generate compound words.	1: Write speech bubbles to describe for characters. 2 & 3*: Use story planner to summarize plot. 4: Use capital letters and spelling days of the week.	Groups 2 & 3 share their work to generate recall of story.
HOUR 3	Read 'The Baker's Cat' on page 82 on top of page 85. Invite prediction. Then read to end and check predictions.	Identify examples of sequencing words from story (eg: 'first', 'then', 'by now', 'finally'). Brainstorm others and write them up for a class resource.	1: Dictionary and thesaurus work. 2 & 3*: Guided re-read of story followed by comprehension questions. 4: Use description of cat on page 83 to draw picture.	Discuss how author lays clues at the beginning of the story about what is going to happen.
HOUR 4	Read 'A Bed for the Night' on page 93 up to the question on page 94. Recall story, identifying characters, setting and problem.	Choose passage from story for a cloze procedure activity, predicting words from grammatical context.	1*: Guided re-read of story, followed by comprehension questions. 2 & 3: Cloze activity practising skills work. 4*: Guided re-read looking for who characters met and in what order.	Discussion on cumulative structure of story. What other stories do the children know with a similar structure?
HOUR 5	Look at the book as a whole and ask pupils to describe it – ie, a book of short stories, all by the same author, fantasy genre etc.	Explore illustrations and elicit pupils' responses. Discuss how illustrations add to or support text (eg: use of colour/black and white reflects everyday life mixed with fantasy).	1: Find other books by same author and compare/contrast. 2 & 3*: Choose a story and read aloud as a play. 4: Choose an illustration and write why they like it.	Select two pupils from Group 4 to read their writing. Ask Group 1 to recommend another Joan Aiken book for further reading.